PENGUIN BOOKS
LET'S BUILD A COMPANY

Harpreet S. Grover and Vibhore Goyal are friends who first met as room-mates at IIT Bombay. They fought a lot, survived each other, and decided that was enough qualification to start a company together. They ran CoCubes.com along with a brilliant team over ten years, before being acquired by Aon Hewitt in an all-cash deal. At the time of acquisition, CoCubes had touched 3 million students across India and worked with 1000+ corporates and colleges.

Harpreet is an active angel investor—some of his deals include Chaayos, ShopKirana and Avail Finance, among others. He witnessed the journey of Ola Cabs closely from before the time it started. Beyond work, Harpreet is a mountaineer and ultra hill runner. He lives with his wife, Bhakti, and daughter, Diya, in Mumbai. He is passionate about helping people figure out how to pursue their interests and abilities.

Vibhore is a business-product guy who loves flying. Post selling CoCubes, he pursued that interest and received a private pilot's licence. Alongside building CoCubes over the years, he co-founded Babajob and filed seven international patents during a thirteen-month stint at Microsoft R & D. He is now the founder and CEO of OneBanc, a fintech start-up. He lives with his wife, Jasjit, in Gurgaon. (Jasjit happens to be Harpreet's cousin, so it is a complicated relationship now, but they are surviving!)

Harpreet tweets at @hsgrover and Vibhore does not tweet at @vibhore_goyal.

ADVANCE PRAISE FOR THE BOOK

'The CoCubes journey will enrich the reader with an honest, on-the-ground perspective of starting a company and managing the ups and downs of entrepreneurship. It is a story of friendship, ambition, pragmatism, empathy and inspiration! Harpreet and Vibhore were my seniors in college, and they were inspirations for many, including me, to take the path of entrepreneurship. This book, I hope, inspires many more!'—Bhavish Aggarwal, founder and chairman, Ola

'As a first-generation entrepreneur, Harpreet's narrative will inspire many young people. He has a lovely style that makes his book very readable. He comes across [as] authentic. Tells you the stuff the way it really is. In parts tough, in parts full of hope, he tells you the story of an enterprise with the ease of a master storyteller. Harpreet is a great writer; visual, evocative, riveting, romantic. This book blurs the line between non-fiction and fiction in style and literary appeal'—Subroto Bagchi, Indian entrepreneur, business leader and author

'Harpreet and Vibhore's journey is like a textbook in entrepreneurship and is a must-read for both young founders and wannabe founders. This straight-from-the-heart account of CoCubes, which I only had a chance to watch from a distance, is peppered with lessons that will help young founders learn about how entrepreneurship truly works—[the book] is not an account of overnight success but the travails of the founders in taking something from idea to exit with all the drama along the way!'—G.V. Ravishankar, managing director, Sequoia

'An authentic account of an entrepreneurial journey'—Sanjeev Bikhchandani, founder and executive vice chairman, Info Edge (Naukri.com)

'A well-articulated narrative by Harpreet Grover and Vibhore Goyal, covering the struggles, triumphs and lessons learnt. As a first-time successful start-up, it makes [for] a very engaging read with quite a few takeaways'—S. Ramadorai, former CEO and MD, Tata Consultancy Services

'Along with the ups and downs of a start-up, the book offers great reflection on how hiring dilutes culture and on managing complex relationships within a company'—R. Swaminathan, chief people officer, WNS Global Services

'This is a story with real titbits that make the journey seem personal. As a reader who wonders what it takes to build a company from scratch, I loved reading what goes on in the mind of an entrepreneur'—Anandorup Ghose, partner, Deloitte

'The journey of entrepreneurship is challenging, exhilarating and rewarding. The CoCubes story embodies all these aspects and makes for a fascinating and inspiring read for anyone interested in or pursuing entrepreneurship'—Kunal Bahl, co-founder and CEO, Snapdeal

'I thought I would read the book over a few days, but then I found I couldn't put it down and read [from] cover to cover in a day! A must-read for first-time entrepreneurs as Happy [Harpreet] and Vibhore's CoCubes story is very relatable and the easy-going writing style makes one feel that one is actually present! I found the second half of the book very interesting, when Happy shares his life and company-building lessons with an intimate look behind the scenes of the journey. [A] very refreshing and unique read which entrepreneurs will enjoy'—Avnish Bajaj, founder and managing partner, Matrix

'*Let's Build a Company* is a candid commentary on the joy, heartache and journey of the rollercoaster ride that is start-up life. Happy and Vibhore are relatable entrepreneurs and their well-captured journey and relatable experiences are a great summation of the people they are and what they set out to build!'—Rohan Malhotra and Arjun Malhotra, founders, Good Capital

'Having been one of the earliest founders in the tech start-up ecosystem, the authors have presented their valuable entrepreneurial experience from ground zero in a manner that any reader will benefit from the same'—Anand Lunia, founding partner, India Quotient

LET'S
BUILD
A COMPANY

A START-UP STORY MINUS THE BULLSHIT

HARPREET S. GROVER
VIBHORE GOYAL

PENGUIN BOOKS

An imprint of Penguin Random House

PENGUIN BOOKS

USA | Canada | UK | Ireland | Australia
New Zealand | India | South Africa | China | Singapore

Penguin Books is part of the Penguin Random House group of companies
whose addresses can be found at global.penguinrandomhouse.com

Published by Penguin Random House India Pvt. Ltd
4th Floor, Capital Tower 1, MG Road,
Gurugram 122 002, Haryana, India

Penguin
Random House
India

First published in Penguin Books by Penguin Random House India 2020

Copyright © Harpreet S. Grover and Vibhore Goyal 2020

ISBN 9780143449836

Typeset in Adobe Caslon Pro by Manipal Technologies Limited, Manipal

Printed at Manipal Technologies Limited, India

www.penguin.co.in

MIX
Paper from
responsible sources
FSC® C043100

Harpreet S. Grover . Vibhore Goyal . Ankur Jindal .
Sameer Nagpal . Manpreet Kaur . Srikanth Reddy .
Himanshu Dixit . Nilay Kothari . Avirup Das . Shashank
Shekhar Mishra . B. Giridhar Mohan . Nishant Ahuja .
Tarun Sharma . Rohit Kumar . Vinay Singh . Naina Gupta .
Ranjit Singh . B. Prashanth Shet . Ishita Mehta . Prerna
Kakkar . Deepti Sengar . Prakash Singh Rawat . Munmun
Sinha . Mradul Sharma . Nitya Nair . Parag Ghatpande .
Amber Nigam . Aakash Roy . Vikas Bhadoaria . Dhruv
Mathur . Kunal Bedarkar . Puneet Ahuja . Chinmoy Dhali .
Arijit Paul . Shipra Ghatpande . Abhyudya Sharma .
Sarthak Barwa . Dharmendra Chauhan . Lovish Khatri .
Karan Parpyani . Gaurav Namdev . Amit Das . Suraj
Narayan . Sahin Sadik . Amit Singh . Pradeep Kumar .
Bandhav Bhatia . Ajoobi Srivastava . Jaun Abbas . Nidhi
Dad . Nisha Ganeriwal . Rohan Bhardwaj . Monica Tyagi .
Anvita Misra . Surinder Kaur . Rajeev Sharma . Abhishek
Jain . Farhan Hafiz . Avisek Chakraborty . Hasmeet Sapra .
Kamal Kishore . Ajay Kumar . Nikhil Pateriya . Chhaviraj .
Geeta Gandhi . Rahul Gupta . Harmeet Kaur . Tanya Joshi .
Rahul Yadav . Manpreet Singh Saini . Naman Khatri .
Dinesh Kumar Gupta . Somil Shrivastava . Ricky Sur .
Rishabh Saxena . Sonal Matta . Disha Kashyap . Rajul Goel .
Nitin Soni . Sanjay Kumar Jaiswal . Aravindan S. Rahul
Pant . Prerna Nandle . Samiksha Sharma . Rahul Pandey .

Anupam Bhandarkar . Siddharth Jamle . Akhtar Ahmed .
Divya Prabha . Guruprasad Shetty . Rajeend Kunnil . Sanjay
Arora . Naman Ahuja . Hasan Fuaad Sadaq . Soumava
Naskar . Jayanth Balamurugan . Chaitanya Saxena .
Jyotsna Singh Chauhan . Alok Rustagi . Anuj . Himanshi
Mukhija . Pushpa Pandit . V. Shriram . Sumanta Guha .
Utkarsh Mishra . Satish Bedre . Anupama Garg . Manish
Sharma . Manish Mirchandani . Amanjeet Saluja . Vibhooti
Kayastha . Gulshan Thakur . Syam Chand . Rahul Kumar .
Nabil Ahmad . Aditi Das . Sugitha Mohan . Akshay Seth .
Avinava Srivastava . Pratik Marwah . Gurpreet Singh . Kunal
Seth . Rahul Choudhary . Yash Girdhar . Aakriti Mehrotra .
Ashok Shankar . Zuhaib Ahmed .

**This book is dedicated to the team members of CoCubes.
You worked harder than us and made everything possible.**

Vishal Gupta . Saurabh Mukerjee . Utpala Ghosh . Deepak
Chawla . Prabhjot Singh Khera . Nishat Farhat . Sanchay
Karidhal . Brajesh Kumar Sen . Amonika Saini . Vijay
Krishna Ramanathan . Suvendu Das . S. Kavitha Reddy .
Punit Sahni . Manas Virmani . Jugal Kishore . Aastha
Bansal . Smrati Awasthi . Bittu Kumar . Neelesh Saxena .
Manik Singh . Apoorva Baranwal . Anand Subramanian .
Maanas Pratap Singh . Ajay Vishnu . Rohit Garg . Veronica
Joseph . Rahul Chaggar . A. Jude Felix . Saurabh Misra .
Gurmeet Singh Walia . Surabhi Ganguly . Abhishek Shahi .
Vijay Kondi . Abhishek Mishra . Punya Anand . Ranjitha
Balla . Ankur Tiwari . Vinod Gupta . Sneha Singh . Aun
Ahmed . Abhimanyu Dubey . Umang Dutta . Hinam
Verma . Vaisakh Sarma . Manda Santoshi . Garima Arora .

J J Raja Neelam . Easha Gupta . Shobhit Dwivedi . Tanpreet
Kaur . Arush Anand . Shivani Gupta . Mayank Tiwari .
Alka Saraf . Ankit Adlakha . Ekta Bathla . Abhijit Kumar .
Nidhi Mota . Divya Adlakha . Ishan Sodhi . Srikanth
Reddy Ragiri . Jasmeet Singh . Anirban Hazra . Jai Prakash .
Y.Sathish Kumar . Rohit Guglani . Hiteshi Dutta .
U. Balamurugan . Vandana Devi . Madda Vikram . Vikram
Singh . Mohit Sharma . Kushagra Jha . Shiva Nagoti . Bharat
Khanna . Bandi Sai Krishna . Prabhjyot Virdi Chhabra .
Mohammed Muiz Musba . Aravind Kumar Patil . Archit
Agarwal . Rahul Agarwal . Shikhar Srivastava . Dipanjana
Bhattacharyya . Gurpreet Saluja . Prashant Gupta . Deepa
Pillai . Pranshu Arora . Rajdeep Singh Parmar . Ashwin
Kini . Aashoo Shukla . Aarti Pajan . Revanth Maturi .
Peeyush Srivastava . Mayank Upadhayay . Navneet Kaur .
Mansi Bhat . Vaibhav Tyagi . Siddharth Rawat . Aarushi
Goyal . Kaushik Sarkar . Ujval Bucha . Deeksha Dhingra .
Anshul Singh . Tulika Aggarwal . Vipul Grover .
Karanpreet Singh Chawla .

*The above names are listed in the order of the total time a team member spent
at CoCubes, with the cut-off taken as the date on which we sold CoCubes to
Aon Hewitt.*

A regret from CoCubes is that we couldn't fully achieve what we really wanted to—provide equal opportunities to students from every college. We underestimated the bureaucracy prevalent in large corporate hiring from colleges, which generally dictates that only students from certain colleges can be hired by that company. As the higher-education system changes, we continue to hope that this will change in the years to come.

contents

PART II: FOR THE ENTREPRENEUR IN YOU

A. Personal Life

B. The Biggest Asset: People

C. Some Learnings

list of abbreviations

BE	Below expectation
BPO	Business process outsourcing
CA	Chartered accountant
DD	Due diligence
EBITDA	Earnings before interest, taxes, depreciation and amortization
EE	Exceeds expectation
ESOP	Employee stock ownership plan
GDP	Gross domestic product
HRO	Human resource outsourcing
IDC	Industrial Design Centre
KRA	Key responsibility area
LoI	Letter of intent
LP	Limited partnership
M&A	Mergers and acquisitions
ME	Meets expectation
P&L	Profit-and-loss statement

Q1	The first quarter of a financial year (January, February and March)
Q2	The second quarter of a financial year (April, May and June)
Q3	The third quarter of a financial year (July, August and September)
Q4	The fourth quarter of a financial year (October, November and December)
RFP	Request for proposal
RS	Rockstar
SHA	Shareholders' agreement
SPA	Share purchase agreement
VC	Venture capitalist

acknowledgements

This is the last page of the book. No, not for you, the reader, but for us, the writers. And it's time to thank all the folks who helped us on our journey.

We want to thank our parents for getting us to the stage where we got into the same college. We should thank our good fortune that we became room-mates.

This book wouldn't have been possible without CoCubes in the first place. So we want to thank all the colleagues and clients we contacted to help us jog our memory about what had really happened during our journey, and remind us of the events, as viewed from their eyes. Our thanks to TiE (The Indus Entrepreneurs) for being the first pit stop for us to learn about entrepreneurship. Thank you to Amanjeet Saluja, who was the first angel to invest money in CoCubes, and to Rajeev Raghunandan and Nikesh Shah, who joined him. A big thanks to Raghu Batta and Gautam Balijepalli for believing in us, giving us our first venture capital and for eventually becoming our friends. To the entire team at Ojas for supporting us when we were down. A note of thanks to Manish Mirchandani, for joining us for a part of the journey. A high five to Sameer Nagpal, without whom the journey wouldn't have been the same, for both of us. Thank you to T.V.G. Krishnamurty, who played a bigger part in this journey than he would ever acknowledge.

The amount of time we spent at CoCubes wouldn't have been possible without us having stolen it in the first place from our respective wives. So, Bhakti and Jasjit, thank you for bearing with us!

We want to thank our friend Farooq (founder, Fynd), for pushing us to write the book. And Ambi M.G. Parameswaran (founder, Brand-Building.com), for introducing us to Anish Chandy (founder, Labyrinth Literary Agency), who agreed to represent the book. Thank you to the team at Penguin: Manasi Subramaniam, for seeing potential in the five chapters we submitted to you; Anushree Majumdar, for being our first 'unofficial editor'; Rachita Raj, for doing it officially and being so patient with all our grammar mistakes while never pointing them out; and Aparna Kumar, for tying it all together and making it work.

We would have definitely missed names here; for that we hope the rest of you can forgive us. Thank you for that!

Cheers,
Vibhore and Harpreet

authors' note

Our friend Farooq Adam (founder of Fynd, now acquired by Reliance) pushed us to write this book. We say 'pushed' because he actually tried pretty hard. We refused. He pushed again. We refused. Then he asked why. We said we hadn't done enough in our lives to write a book. And he said, 'Happy [as I am generally called by friends], everyone can take that stand at any point in time. We can all move forward and not write about our journey. But then how will we share what we have learnt?' That made sense to me. He introduced us to Anish Chandy (the founder of Labyrinth Literary Agency and now my agent), who heard me out politely. Then he paused and said, 'Hmm, I like your story because it seems believable. Anyone who reads a book on building a billion-dollar company might not believe that they will build it. But by reading yours, they can believe they can do it too.'

Vibhore and I had spent ten years building CoCubes. We had started with the idea of raising a lot of venture capital and building a billion-dollar company. And we had ended up building a profitable company which was sold for cash to the largest HR consulting firm in the world. It had taken time, but it had happened, and everyone associated with the company had made money—the team members, the angel investors and the venture capitalists. It was a positive outcome overall.

So we sat down to write the book. While I did the writing (it was easier that way than both of us trying to write)—on account of which the book is in my words—Vibhore, with his razor-sharp memory, kept me honest about how the events had actually unfolded. So this book is written in the first person, but it reflects our collective experience.

As first-time writers, we received a lot of advice. Some solicited, some unsolicited. Some we followed, some we didn't. One piece of advice we consistently got was to have a summary in bullet points at the end of each chapter. This was something we didn't want to do at all. We never liked anyone telling us: *Here are the five takeaways for you.* If the gist is in the bullet points at the end, why write the chapter? We think the bullets miss the point. We believe that every reader is on their own journey. And as you read a book, there are no fixed takeaways. Where you are on your journey will determine your relationship with the book. If you are going through a rough phase in your business, your relationship will be a certain way. If you are a college student looking to start a company, your relationship will be another way. These relationships can't be summed up in bullet points. So this book doesn't have 'learnings' at the end of the chapters.

While writing, we realized what a humongous effort it was to put pen to paper. And our respect for every book writer out there grew.

The book is written in two parts. The first part is the story of building CoCubes. This is the true story of how our company was built. The second part shares how we did that and our takeaways. Picking up a newspaper to read about funding rounds seems glitzy, but the life of an entrepreneur is not easy. Entrepreneurship takes a toll on one's personal life, and a few chapters in the second half share learnings from this aspect of our journey.

I hope you become friends with this book, and it makes you feel that you can do whatever it is that you wish to accomplish; that if you really want to, you can build a company.

introduction

Life after Selling the Company

CoCubes was a company Vibhore and I started in Gurgaon in 2007 and exited in 2019 to Aon, a global professional services firm. The name 'CoCubes' comes from the first two letters of three words: connecting, colleges and companies. Over the years, we morphed into an online assessment company, which means we created tests for hiring. If a large company wanted to filter applications before interviews, they used our online assessments to do so. If a graduate wanted to find a job, he or she took our standardized online test, which gave them direct access to interviews in a lot of companies that were hiring. This was our simple business.

After selling CoCubes to Aon, I asked my wife, Bhakti, what she wanted to do. She had spent the last ten years in the shadow of CoCubes. She had moved to Gurgaon and taken up a job there because CoCubes was located in Gurgaon.

She said she wanted to live in Mumbai for some time. I said, 'Okay, why don't you find a job there?' I had thought it would take six months to get a good job opportunity. But in only two weeks, Bhakti had got a job at Nomura, and in six weeks we had moved to Mumbai! (I realized after this that I must never challenge my wife.) Aon was accommodating of the request. Given that the CoCubes head office was still in Gurgaon, I used to travel each week to meet the team. And since the leadership team had been in CoCubes for a long time, communication was easy.

Our deal with Aon was structured in such a way that we had a two-year 'golden handcuff' period, which meant that if we stayed with Aon for two years, we would get a large payout. Also, we had annual targets to meet, which, if met, would make all the shareholders a lot of money. We were clear with Aon, and with the leadership team, that we would stay for two years and look to move after that. Because that is why we had sold the company in the first place. We wanted to build a billion-dollar company. And CoCubes didn't seem to be headed in that direction. Hence, we sold it. It gave us a big financial cushion and set us up for the future.

When we were close to selling the company, I had met an acquaintance who had sold his company to LinkedIn for a few hundred crores. I asked him what really changed after selling the company. He replied that he didn't need to worry about spending small bits of money. That he wouldn't care about the food bill in the restaurant, or be okay with paying for a seat with more leg space on a flight. Everything else remained the same.

Vibhore and I agree on this. This is something that really changes—the knowledge that you won't run out of money by spending it as change. So that cognitive load of keeping a tab on small expenses goes away.

Another change was that now we had to manage our money. This was a new thing. We had barely had any money in our accounts earlier. I remember going to the ATM in 2013 to withdraw 2000 bucks and realizing I couldn't. And now all the wealth managers in India were writing and calling. For the first year we thought this could be outsourced. That someone else could manage our money for us. But the bad first-year results told us that money management was a new skill that we would need to learn. This journey of spending time researching on the best way to grow money has been interesting. It was while reading about this that I came across this quotation, 'Seek wealth, not money.' What the person meant was that one should seek an asset which continues to grow and give you money, rather than money itself. I remember reading it and thinking that that asset was CoCubes, but we had traded it for hard cash!

Both of us now also had time on our hands. We tried to catch up with our friends but realized that they were still busy. So even though we had time, our frequency of meeting friends wasn't really increasing. That's when we shifted our focus to doing some things we had both wanted to do for a long time.

Vibhore wanted to learn flying. So he used the last three years to learn how to fly a Cessna plane and get a pilot's licence.

I have been doing mountaineering for the last ten years. In 2006, by sheer luck, I joined a bunch of friends on an expedition to Kalindikhal Pass—a treacherous pass at a 6000-metre altitude, surrounded by glaciers. This was the most beautiful landscape I had ever seen. It was physically tiring but life-changing. I was hooked. I wanted to climb 8000-metre peaks. But that needed money. Climbing an 8000-metre peak (including Everest) with a reputed agency can cost up to Rs 60 lakh. After selling CoCubes, I had the money to pursue that path.

Over the next two years I went to Dhaulagiri (the world's seventh-highest mountain) on a fifty-day expedition and started doing ultra hill-running, competing in 100-km races.

While Vibhore continued to stay engaged in work, I personally stepped back from getting too involved. Being in Mumbai, away from the head office, helped too. I spent a lot of time reading and with my four-year-old daughter.

A lot has changed in the ten years that we built CoCubes. What hasn't changed is the concern a parent has for their child in India. As we left CoCubes in April 2019, thinking we would take a few months off to chill and relax, our moms started calling us daily to ask, '*Beta*, what are you planning to do next?'

So here's to middle-class values. And to living a life where we work on something we love.

And to all of you, all the best.

PART I

STARTING A START-UP

one

the idea of cocubes

I started my first business in the fourth standard—with no funding, in my dad's scooter garage.

Back in 1990, four-storey buildings in our neighbourhood in Pitampura, west Delhi, used to have scooter garages; small spaces that could just about fit in a scooter and a cycle. All my pocket money went into renting *Super Commando Dhruv*, *Nagraj*, *Bankelal* and all the other Hindi comics that were popular then. I had a friend who was couple of years older, and we would rent comics together and then swap them. Once a month, our parents would also let us buy some.

Between the two of us, we had about fifty comics, which, we soon realized, were more than what the shopkeeper had in stock at any given point in time. An idea hit us: why not give out our comics on rent and make some pocket money? The shopkeeper loaned them out for Rs 1 a day, and we could charge half the rate. We had no bills to pay, no family to feed. We just wanted some pocket money. So I asked my dad to take his scooter out of the garage and thus began our comic-book business! We had almost every kid in the neighbourhood coming to us to rent comics. It went on well for about three months. Then my dad got transferred to another government-bank branch in Patiala and our business had to shut down. That was my first taste of what I would later realize is termed 'entrepreneurship'.

While I was growing up in Patiala, Vibhore was failing seventh-standard maths. His parents decided that he needed to get coaching to ensure he cleared his exams. They also wanted him to learn the value of hard work. So Vibhore started working in a garage, repairing bikes to earn pocket money. As he grew older, his fondness for computers grew and, along with school, he started teaching C++ in a local coaching centre. (By the time he got to college, he knew more coding than final-year computer science graduates. This would really come in handy when he helped me clear our first-year course in Fortran.)

Cut to 2000, when I was accepted into IIT Bombay, a letter came home stating that all first-year students would have to share a room. I thought it would be a good idea to reach a couple of days in advance and take the best of the two beds. When I arrived, I found this geeky guy already there with his trunk placed below the better bed. Vibhore Goyal had beaten me to it and set the tone of our friendship for years to come.

Both of us had enrolled in the five-year dual degree civil-engineering programme. While Vibhore was disappointed with his rank (he had hoped to crack the top 100), I was delighted just to get in. But now that we were in, both of us wanted to change our branch of study. There was just one hitch—in our branch, there were fourteen students, and the institute's rule stipulated that not more than 10 per cent of the branch could proceed to switch courses, meaning, only one of us could actually succeed. We agreed to be on friendly terms as both of us worked hard to get our branch changed. But after one semester, Vibhore got 9.7/10 while I had 7.3/10, and I decided it was best to let him win.[1] I was quite happy with civil engineering. We spent a year together in room number 143 of Hostel Three. While Vibhore chose to spend his time studying, I spent my time outdoors. I tried teaching him table tennis while he tried explaining how mathematical equations worked. Both of us failed. But come what may, we ensured we always ate dinner together. Irrespective of how hungry we were, we would wait for each other. We never said that we would do this, it just became a habit.

The five years at IIT Bombay were eventful and we ended up spending a lot of time together. From the second year onwards, Vibhore had a bike, which I would borrow—only to slip on the road and smash the headlight. We would then go together to get it repaired. In the third year, Vibhore got an internship in Pune; I went to meet him on the last day so that we could lug his computer back together—he drove the bike back to the institute while I sat behind holding a big CPU between us on a wet highway. Another thing we always did was go to the station to drop the first person who was going home at the end of semester. Vibhore's parents would send him an AC first-class ticket, and he would find someone to sell it to. He would then buy a general ticket to go to Jaipur and pocket the rest. I always found this funny, not to mention enterprising.

By the time we graduated, Vibhore had spent time working on a high-tech start-up based out of IIT Bombay and landed a job with Microsoft's research division. Meanwhile, I had tried to start a brand for fresh fruit juice with my classmates Ritesh and Rahul, and failed. We bought a mixer but trying to figure out the economics of how many carrots provided one glass of juice proved to be too much trouble. I finally landed a job in Inductis, a data analytics company. After the final interviews, the company took us to a five-star for a buffet. There, they asked me if I already knew all the questions they had posed in the interview. Apparently, I had the highest score across interviews. I said no. They said, then you are quite stupid, because we asked the same questions we asked last year. That got my mind buzzing and I spent most of my final year creating a document titled 'BePrepared', which was a compilation of interview experiences of final-year students.

While together in IIT, Vibhore and I had discussed starting a company, but our ideas were always up in the air. Also, it was clear in our minds that we wanted to get a job after graduation. After all, that's why we had come to IIT in the first place.

2006: Mid-Job Crisis

One year into the job and I was itching for a change. So I used my newly developed PowerPoint skills and made a deck called 'Ideas 1.0'. I listed down all the opportunities that I thought were worth pursuing. The list contained an idea for an online food-delivery service (we were bachelors and food delivered home, especially late at night, was always welcome). Another idea was called 'Lifeinlines'—so that one could continuously update about one's life on an online timeline in short sentences.

(I like to think of it as the original Twitter, but I will let it slide.) Then there was a consumer-complaint forum and, finally, a slide for an idea that would eventually become CoCubes.

This slide had come about because of an incident that had taken place some time back.

I was sitting at my desk in Inductis when my Reliance phone rang. It was my mom at the other end. She said, 'Beta, this uncle is in Gurgaon and he wants to meet you today.' Well, who likes meeting relatives? But then who can say no to their mother in India? So I met my uncle, and he asked me to introduce him to the HR at Inductis. When I asked him why, he said, 'I am a placement officer at a college in Sangrur and I want to invite your company to come to our campus.' I introduced him to the HR person; they spoke for a little while and then he left. And I forgot about the incident.

Three months later, I bumped into my uncle at a family function. I asked him if anything came out of that meeting. He then told me that he travels to Delhi, Mumbai, Chennai and other major cities, meets the HR department in several companies and asks them to visit the campus. Everyone says yes but nobody ever does. I went back to my HR guy and asked him his view. He said, 'Harpreet, your uncle's college is 300 km away from Gurgaon. If I go all the way and am unable to hire anybody, I will lose my job.' I went back to my desk and searched online. From 2000–05, the number of private colleges in India had gone through the roof. There were 34,000 colleges, and most of them were in tier-2 and tier-3 cities. But all the employers were in the metros, and there seemed to be no way to connect the two sides. This was a problem worth solving.

Vibhore and I used to be in touch mostly through email; we would get on a call only once a month. When we spoke, we discussed starting a company together and brainstormed ideas. He was mostly in the US and getting a hold of him could be difficult.

As soon as the idea of how a platform could connect colleges and companies came up, I called Vibhore. And CoCubes was born over the phone. The name comes from the first two letters of three words—connecting, colleges and companies. Co x Co x Co makes CoCubes.

The only other serious contender for the name we considered was jointcampus.com. I am happy that we didn't pick it. It's a terrible name. It would have limited our company to a specific concept within a broader market.

I think we chose to pursue CoCubes because we were close to the problem as individuals. We had just graduated and had seen the placement cycle, and it seemed like a real problem to solve. Also, the larger purpose of bringing equal opportunities to all students in India appealed to us. These students never got the chance because they were considered as one entity, as a college. We wanted to change that and help individual, skilled students become visible and have the same access and opportunity as someone in a good college.

Initially, for CoCubes, I told Vibhore that we should just collect the résumés of all college students and then sell these to corporates. But better sense prevailed and we chose to use technology to solve the problem. As we discussed, we realized that for a fresh graduate, actually, a résumé did not matter at all. Because, more often than not, there was nothing concrete to write in there.

To thrash out the idea of CoCubes, I flew to Hyderabad to spend two days to make the schema. We camped at Dhayan's place. Dhayan and I had worked together closely for

IIT Bombay's Techfest, Asia's largest science and technology festival. I was the publicity manager and Dhayan was our star designer from IDC (Industrial Design Centre at IIT Bombay). We spent two days dissecting the idea, designing the logo, thinking about user flows, etc. All three of us were keen on the idea.

As we went back to our jobs, progress was slow. But we seemed to be going somewhere. Then all of a sudden, Vibhore vanished. I tried reaching out to him over email and tried his phone number. But I didn't hear back. This went on for a couple of months, and I thought the bastard had ditched me. The excitement of starting CoCubes was dying as Vibhore and I were unable to touch base. Then one night my phone rang. It was a US number. Vibhore. Before I could shout at him, he said, 'I have quit my job at Microsoft. I am landing tomorrow morning in Delhi. Let us start CoCubes.'

Now, it was my turn to leave my job. Dhayan decided that this was too risky for him to do but promised to help while keeping his old job.

I didn't resign immediately. At Inductis, my 'retention bonus' of Rs 2 lakh was due in two months. I decided to wait for it, as that would be the seed money to start the company. Also, I thought it would be best to go and meet actual customers before putting in my papers. So I went to Chandigarh, picked up my Dad's Maruti 800 and visited all the colleges in the area. I ended up meeting placement officers and the chairmen in most of the colleges. All the places I visited showed a lot of interest in CoCubes. So I went back to Gurgaon and quit my job.

Every middle-class parent aspires to see their son or daughter do better than them. To progress in life, earn money, have a stable life. So when we told our parents about leaving our jobs, they were dead against it. They couldn't understand why, after all the hard work of getting into an IIT, after actually getting a job and earning well, we would ditch all of it. In our minds, however, we were clear. If the start-up didn't work, we had the skills to find another job. It might, at worst, mean a setback of a few years, but in the long run it wouldn't matter. I had always believed in living life with no regrets; I didn't want to be forty years old and think I could have done this or that at twenty-four. I wanted to be twenty-four and doing it.

I think, in India, one's relationship with their parents is quite funny. First, they oppose you, but if they see that you are hell-bent on doing something, they capitulate and become your biggest supporters. This is what happened to us. We were finally on our way to building CoCubes.

two

becoming an entrepreneur

Becoming an entrepreneur is one of the most humbling experiences one can have. Most folks who are not entrepreneurs equate it with seeing one's name in the newspaper, giving a media interview, raising large rounds of funding and having a nice office and people to do the work. It is the exact opposite of this picture. Early-stage entrepreneurship is about waiting at the reception of your client's office, going to conferences and trying to make contacts, then following up with them to get meetings, hoping they remember you, trying to convince people to join your start-up and then figuring out, each month, how to pay salaries. This is what will mostly happen when you start a company.

After quitting my job, I returned to the same colleges in Chandigarh. Nobody signed up. Suddenly, they wanted to know which companies we were working with and what we would do with the student data—apart from many other questions. This incident always summarizes entrepreneurship for me. For the most part, this is the life of an entrepreneur: trying to thread a needle in this ever-changing world.

But now that we had left our jobs, there was nothing more to do than to go about building the company. We had to decide where to start Gurgaon, where I was based; or Bangalore, where Vibhore was. Finally, we decided on Gurgaon as it was midway between Jaipur and Chandigarh, his home town and mine, respectively. Vibhore moved to Gurgaon and we started CoCubes by incorporating the company in August 2007 in Chandigarh, the only place where we knew a chartered accountant.

Shaking off the 'Smartness Syndrome'

My first and only job after college had been with Inductis. Most of the people it hired were from top-tier colleges. The company and the people who worked there, including myself, took pride in the fact that we took up difficult projects and solved complex problem for our clients. When we got a simple project, we argued that the company was diluting its brand by doing such projects. The culture in the company promoted the same thought—that we were a high-end data analytics firm.

In 2004, a company called Mu Sigma was founded; they offered data analytics services as well. But the projects were simple ones and generally long-term contracts. This meant that once they won a project from a client, it was easy to execute it and the project provided revenue over multiple years. Mu Sigma became India's first profitable unicorn and is still going strong. Inductis, meanwhile, was sold for about 20 million dollars to EXL in 2006.

Inductis was founded in 2000 and had ample opportunity to do what Mu Sigma had done. But the culture there was one where smartness was overvalued. Smart people are difficult to hire and even more difficult to retain. There are only a few companies solving complex problems, so complex projects are fewer in number. And solving complex problems doesn't generate repeat business.

When I shifted from being an employee to starting my own company, I realized one thing: many companies which build a big and profitable business generally solve the simplest of problems. Their problem statements are clear and repeatable. Solving difficult problems gave us a natural high, one which we had become accustomed to. As I gradually became an entrepreneur, I wanted to really shake that off and get on the road.

Initial Idea

Our initial bare-bones idea was simple enough: we wanted to go to colleges and ask the students to come online. We would get the initial ones for free and then start asking for money. At that time, the source of information for a corporate was only what the placement officer told them. But quite often that was off by a wide margin because the placement officer had no real way of getting that confirmation from students and could only collate email responses. Plus, the placement officer wanted the company to visit, so they would always overstate the numbers. We wanted to build a platform for corporates, encouraging visibility in the campus-hiring process, so that before they travelled to the institute, they would exactly know how many students had applied for a job in their company.

And by using our SMS service, they could engage with the students as well.

Being Naive

When we began, we were two years out of college and didn't know any corporates. So we reached out to our network of friends who were employed in different companies and sought their help. All those folks stepped forward and helped us out by introducing us to the HR department in their companies.

One of our first introductions was to Birlasoft, a mid-sized IT services company. I generally dedicated the first half of the day to reaching out to new clients. One morning, I spoke to the head of recruitment at Birlasoft on the phone, using my friend's reference, and requested a meeting. He politely listened to me and said sure. I looked at my watch and saw it was noon. Birlasoft's office was in Noida, and I still had to take a shower. So I asked him if I could come and meet him at 2 p.m. I think I heard a small choke at the other end, after which he politely suggested that I write him an email and that he'd get back to me, if he had the time, by next week. I felt that the world was conspiring against us to slow us down. Here we were, two guys who had left their jobs to start a company, trying to run as fast as we could, and the world was just not interested in matching our pace. But this was a good lesson on how to schedule corporate meetings, one of many that I learnt as an entrepreneur.

Being Unreasonable

In our pre-final year at IIT, my long-distance relationship with my girlfriend in Patiala ended. She informed me over the phone that she couldn't stay together after three long years, during which we had met only twice. That same night, I boarded a twenty-eight-hour train, sitting in the general coach, and landed up at her house. She politely told me to go back. The following day, I took the twenty-eight-hour train back to IIT. Sometimes, being impulsive and seemingly unreasonable doesn't work. But sometimes it sure does.

A little while into CoCubes, Bhakti (who had become my girlfriend in our final year of college) introduced me to her brother's friend, who was working at Patni, an IT services company. He further introduced us to Geetha, who was the campus head in Patni at that time. She met with us and we had a pleasant interaction. Over the next few months, we took our discussion forward and I ended up meeting Milind, her boss, and the other folks at Patni. Things were going well, and there was a big chance that they could become our first big IT services client. To take things forward, we had verbally agreed to do a pilot together.

Then, one night around 10 p.m., an email landed in my inbox, saying that Patni would not be able to proceed with the pilot due to certain internal reasons. This was a big blow. We were in the middle of trying to raise our venture-capital round and we desperately wanted to move ahead with Patni. It was too late in the night to call Geetha, and I knew that if I called in the morning and asked for reasons, the conversation would only go downhill. So I booked an early-morning flight to Mumbai and wrote Geetha an email saying that we were really looking to add value to Patni's campus-placement process, and that I would be at her office by 9 a.m.

By the time she read the email, I was already on the plane. It was a blind shot. I didn't have an appointment. I had no other meetings lined up. And here I was, spending our limited money on air tickets. Geetha called as soon as she reached office and told me not to come to Mumbai. But by that time, I'd reached the Patni office reception. She came out to meet me and we spent some time together. While I was nervous, I was convinced that we could add value to Patni's campus recruitment. At the end of that meeting, she promised to help find a way to move ahead that year. And we did.

Patni, over time, became one of our biggest clients. Over the years, it was acquired by iGATE, resulting in more business. And then when iGATE got acquired by Capgemini, they became CoCubes's largest client. I think that the decision to take a flight and go was unreasonable. But a start-up is so fragile that nothing less works.

three

getting things done

The word 'jugaad' is often used to signify creativity—to make existing things work or to create new things with meagre resources. One of the key tests for an entrepreneur to succeed is to see if he can get things done. Can he find a way around things and get to the objective? Can he find a way to be efficient about getting to the end goal?

When we started our company, we didn't have many resources. So we resorted to a lot of jugaad.

Reaching Out to Colleges

Today, almost every engineering and MBA college-owner and placement officer knows about CoCubes. When we started in 2007, the name CoCubes was difficult for some to pronounce. In one of the meetings with colleges, an article in a national newspaper referred to us as 'Cokebuzz'. We knew we had to do something to get colleges to take us seriously. So we did some jugaad.

I had been a publicity manager for Techfest, IIT Bombay. We used to send out invitation letters to 800-odd colleges in the country. This contained our poster, an invitation letter and details of the event. For years now, Techfest teams have enjoyed good camaraderie and have always been helpful to each other. So I reached out to the publicity manager of Techfest that year and requested permission to insert a small CoCubes envelope in the overall package that they would send out. He agreed. We printed letters addressed to the directors of the colleges, stating that we were IIT Bombay alumni, and for Rs 15,000 we could bring their entire college online and help increase placements. About 800 envelopes went out. In two weeks, we were swamped with requests for meetings from all over the country. I was the only travelling sales guy. In a couple of months, we had closed one of our first customers— all of this from the mere 2000 bucks we spent on printing a letter on our letterhead.

Getting Our First Clients and Testimonials

Like most other start-ups, we had no credibility when we started, and everyone we met asked us the same question: 'Do you work with someone right now? Is someone using your services?' Saying 'no' would not get us anywhere. So we decided to improvise. Some of my batchmates had started their own companies and they immediately became our first 'customers'. I reached out to my professors too, told them in detail about what we were doing and requested testimonials. A testimonial which read 'CoCubes will be the future of campus recruitment' from an IIT professor would carry some weight, in both colleges as well as companies. Vivek Agarwal, who had been introduced to us by TiE (a Silicon Valley non-profit supporting start-ups) and was now a mentor, became a customer. He also introduced us to his friends, who were okay to help a start-up get off the ground. These first clients and testimonials helped us seem credible in front of real companies and clients!

Getting Meetings with People

Colleges are generally run by influential people—sometimes even by politicians or industrialists. And you can't sign up a college without getting consent from the owner. But getting a meeting with them is not easy. Our sales team continuously tried to find ways to meet the owners of colleges—from trying to find out their morning-walk routine to which brand of cars they liked. In terms of sheer effort, Avirup, our sales guy in Odisha, took the cake. He did some research on a college chairman and found out that he owned a football club. After that, Avirup kept visiting the football club and finally waylaid the chairman when he came for a club meeting there!

In our early days, we hired a programmer called Ramesh Sao.[1] He was our first team member. This was when we were still working out of our houses. He stayed for a few months but was not performing well, so we asked him to leave. But his email ID was active and that gave us an idea. I changed his email signature to that of a sales person. To create the impression of being a bigger company than we were, I would use his email ID to mail prospective clients and ask for a meeting for the CEO (myself). This helped navigate through some of the junior folks and worked well till we found a real sales person.

Renting an Office without Paying Rent

By the first half of 2008, we were a few people strong, and working out of home was proving to be counterproductive. We were looking to raise money and investors wanted to visit the office. Some of our clients had also asked where we were working out of. We seriously started thinking about moving to an office space. But we didn't have money to pay rent. So, in order to find a solution, we met with the directors of all the colleges who were close to our residence. We wanted to convince them that giving us space on the campus was a good idea. For a college, having smart people work out of the campus, supporting a start-up, would create a culture of entrepreneurship. We could help them with some of the internal products that they wanted to develop, organize guest lectures from people in the industry and, eventually, obviously, offer the services of CoCubes. We also offered them equity in CoCubes in exchange for space. It would be a win-win situation for everyone.

We finally found our 'home' at the Ansal Institute of Technology (now Ansal University) in Gurgaon; the director, Dr M.P. Singh, and Prof. Anil Yadav were supportive throughout our stay at the institute. We shared 1 per cent equity with the institute for two years of rent-free space and agreed to pay Rs 30 per sq. ft after that. We spent three wonderful years there, running our start-up from the campus with access to a football ground, a tennis court, the coffee shop and the cafeteria. It was win-win all around.

four

money for our idea

When we chose CoCubes over all the other ideas, we didn't think which one would be the easiest to raise money for. We picked an idea that we believed in and were passionate about. This isn't a very smart thing to do if your key goal is to be wealthy in a short span of time. But choosing an idea that we really believed in and wanted to see established helped us take it to the end.

One of the first things one must do as a young founder is raise money for the start-up. The first round of money is generally 'seed money'. I don't know the origin of the word, but one incident really brought home the reality associated with it. In 2012, CoCubes was well known in the investor circle. But nobody knew that internally we were looking to change the business model—the older model was just not working. It was at that time that I got a meeting with Ganesh Krishnan (the founder of online tutoring firm TutorVista and an angel investor), Meena Ganesh and their partner, Srikanth Iyer. They had sold a majority share in TutorVista to Pearson for 127 million dollars a few months ago,[1] and Ganesh was considered to be a great angel investor to have on board.

We had a great start to the conversation. Srikanth had an interesting analogy to describe why he liked CoCubes. He said that in the US, Facebook became popular, because, for teenagers, dating is a major priority. Now, in India, the thought spinning in most teenagers' heads is leaving college and getting a job. Hence, CoCubes would be required and would become popular. It was a good hypothesis. I used it several times after that, both with investors and clients.

But as the discussion came around to numbers, I mentioned that the next year would see a dip in our revenue. We were tweaking our business model and moving towards profitability. Suddenly, the tone of the discussion changed. It went from hot to cold in five minutes. Ganesh was quite upfront and said that he wouldn't be interested in investing. He said, 'A start-up is like a seed. When an angel investor or a VC is looking at investing in the start-up, the belief is that this seed will lead to a big forest that will bear fruits, which they will pluck. But when it is clear that a particular seed will only lead to a single tree, no one would be interested in investing.' This analogy about 'seed money' has stayed with me ever since.

To many entrepreneurs this analogy might be obvious, but to a lot of entrepreneurs I have met, it is not. They are trying to raise money for their start-up, going from one VC to another, getting rejected and not understanding why. They deeply believe that their start-up has value and that the VC is unable to see it. So they keep iterating their story, keep iterating their pitch deck. They believe that the VC is unable to understand, but the reality is the opposite. The VC fully understands that this will not be a large company, or not large enough for them to make money.

A lot of the times the answer lies in market size. The business the entrepreneur is building may not have a large-enough market size for the VC to be interested. The venture capital industry works on the principle of a seed growing into a large forest. There, money is made by big exits, not by mediocre exits. Big exits mean a company which can return the fund, i.e. if the fund size is 100 million dollars, the VC should be able to see an upside to that tune if everything goes well. Big exits need a large market size. And many markets or business models simply don't cater to that.

One of the main questions that entrepreneurs who are starting off ask is: How do I decide the valuation of my company? What should I say or offer to the investor? How do I decide if the investor is pricing fairly or not? There is no logic to it. It is a matter of supply and demand. If lots of people want your start-up, your valuation will be high. If no one wants it, your valuation will be low. Your start-up is a seed, and the valuation depends on how big someone believes it will become. To make someone believe that, you need to add signals. As you add more positive signals, your valuation increases. It depends on how much you believe it is worth, and as you add more and more signals to show that your start-up can become big, the valuation increases. If your initial product is built, it grows a bit. If you have a few people using it, it grows. If you have paid customers, it grows further. The same principle applies to the entrepreneur. If you are an entrepreneur who has built and sold a company earlier, the starting valuation can be much higher. This is because VCs will line up to offer you money, because there are a lot of positive signals available about you, as you have already started and sold a company.

When Bhavish Aggarwal started cab-hailing service Ola in 2010, and was trying to raise the first round of funding, he went through all the difficulties that a newbie entrepreneur faces. He pitched to folks in coffee shops, he went to all the big funds. Finally, he raised the seed round at a valuation of less than 1 million dollars. The company is now worth more than 6 billion dollars. He was a first-time entrepreneur then, with few signals attached to him. In 2019, he started Ola Electric, raising Rs 400 crore in the first round, with valuation rising to a billion dollars in six months' time. This is the strength of signals.[2]

five

seed and angel money

To start CoCubes, both Vibhore and I had invested Rs 2 lakh each. In a couple of months we had raised seed money of Rs 4 lakh. This was given by Amanjeet Saluja, or Aman, as we call him. He was a vice president at Inductis (my first and only job after college). We gave him 2 per cent equity for this money. He stayed invested in the company till the end and made over a crore when it was sold. My first few meetings with him were not about raising capital. I originally went to him for advice. He helped us think through the problem, did the whiteboarding with us and finally invested after we had left our jobs. I do think that it was a risky investment because of the size of the cheque. It was a little bit of money to get us off the ground and could easily have been burned through in six months. But I think at the earliest stage, the only people who can invest in you are the three Fs: friends, family and fools. Our friends were just out of college, in their first jobs, and our families didn't have a lot of money. So we had to convince someone else! All angel investors are fools in that sense. Because the return on capital invested is rare for most angels.

Aman was also our first coach. I would reach out to him for stuff that seems trivial now. Like talking about whether we should fly down for a conference to Bangalore or not. If yes, should both founders go? We spoke to him when a college we were trying to sign up suggested that we co-brand CoCubes with them for a college event in Punjab, along with giving them exclusive rights for the region. He also jumped on a few client calls with corporate customers, which gave us more credibility than we had. He helped us build the first financial model for CoCubes. I remember that when we had to allocate shares to him, we didn't know how to calculate the number of shares to be given. Should we give him shares from the ones we have, or should we issue new ones? All these things, which seem so familiar now, are part of the learning curve for a new entrepreneur.

Even in 2007, Rs 8 lakh couldn't go very far. But with it we could rent an apartment at Rs 20,000 per month and start working from there. One fine day, as we were sitting in the drawing room of our apartment, my professor from IIT Bombay gave me a call. He said, 'Harpreet, I heard you have started a company. My brother-in-law's brother-in-law [*saale ka saala*] is just graduating from college and is looking for a job. Do speak to him.' I had no option but to say yes.

This is how we were introduced to Ankur Jindal. He was from Moga (a small town in Punjab) and gave me a call. I asked him why he wanted to join a start-up. He said that he wanted to do an MBA and was looking to pass some time to get an experience letter. I said goodbye and promptly called my professor to inform him about the conversation. The following day, Ankur called me back and said he wanted to meet in person. I asked him to come home. When he came over in the evening, we were eating samosas on the dining table. He said there had been a miscommunication and that he was actually very interested in doing a job and learning. Such a change of heart, and soul, in a day! We were anyway looking to hire someone for operations and research, so we asked him to come in from the next day. He asked where he should come. We told him to come to the same location, where else?

When Ankur came the next day, I was in Mumbai for a client meeting. So when he reached home, Vibhore was there, along with Ramesh Sao. Vibhore gave Ankur a laptop and asked him to make himself at home. Ankur thought, *Okay, maybe after this we will go to the office.* After a couple of hours, Vibhore said, 'Let us go out to have coffee.' Ankur thought this was nice. Having coffee with the founder before going to the office. So the three of them went to a nearby Café Coffee Day in Vibhore's car and spent an hour or so there. After that, as they drove back, Ankur saw all the gleaming glass corporate offices, wondering which one the car would stop at. The car eventually stopped at our house. This is when Ankur finally realized where the real office was.

As we grew a few people strong, we continued to approach both college and corporate prospects. I remember one of the first conflicts we had as co-founders was when clients were willing to sign up, but the product was not ready. So I asked, why don't we outsource it rather than building it ourselves? Vibhore patiently explained to me that while that would be faster now, in the long run, as changes come and the product becomes more complex, it would be harmful to the company. It took a big fight between us to resolve that. And for me, to learn that to build a product company for the long run, in-house ownership of product, is better.

In February 2008, I reached out to someone who had just sold his company to one of the largest BPOs in the country. I had met him a couple of times before and wrote a short email sharing that we were now working on CoCubes full time. He was in his late thirties then and had owned most of the shares in his company when it was sold, making more than 15 million dollars in cash (when a dollar used to be equal to about Rs 42). He was keen to know more about CoCubes. He also knew Aman well, which helped. Our first meeting happened in March. Over the course of the next few meetings, the investor offered to introduce us to a few prospective clients and bring in others who could add value. We converted the first prospect we were introduced to in about a month. As the positive signals grew by the end of April, we ended up with a term sheet from him for raising Rs 2 crore at a valuation of Rs 8 crore post-money. Now, as I write this after twelve years of being an entrepreneur, getting a term sheet for half a million dollars in six weeks for a young first-time entrepreneur seems like good progress. But back then, as someone who wanted to get things done fast, it felt awfully slow.

Our investor had been proactive in helping and bringing on board the right mix of other investors. He introduced us to the owner of a large college chain, the HR head of a large BPO and to the owner of a large recruitment firm. We met all of them, and each decided to invest in the round. The lead investor himself had built and sold a company, so that was valuable experience. All good signals except that the term sheet seemed too complex. This was the first term sheet we had ever seen. In our entire batch, there was only one other person, Gagan Goyal, who had raised money so far. He was building a robotics company called Thinklabs, and his term sheet had been simpler.

Aman introduced us to a private equity investor who mentioned that this was a complex term sheet for the early stage and recommended that we get a lawyer who would help us understand it and negotiate. I reached out to other senior entrepreneurs I had met at conferences, to seek their help in understanding the term sheet, and they also suggested the same. So we were introduced to Trilegal, one of the best law firms in the country. What shocked me initially were the fees—it seemed like the bill would shoot up to more than Rs 3 lakh. That was close to 50 per cent of the total money we had in the bank. We agreed on an hourly rate, hoping to use their services as little as possible. I remember checking with Trilegal if we still had to pay if the deal didn't go through for any reason. The answer, obviously, was yes.

Another month went in negotiations, and we came to agree on the term sheet. But then came the shareholders' agreement which turned out to be more complex. Moreover, it had some terms that were not mentioned in the term sheet earlier. It was the end of July by the time we got around to finalizing the SHA. We were running out of money. The investor was quite involved in doing the deal, but we began to realize that an involved investor came with their own set of pros and cons. Our investor had introduced us to a few more college owners and helped us think through our model in terms of profitability by customer size. When we were on the verge of closing our first corporate customer, he introduced us to the country head, so that we had a better chance at the deal. But the investor wanted to be the chairman of CoCubes and also wanted, what we felt, was a lot of financial control once the money had been invested. For example, he had put in the option of the investor being able to liquidate the company if only 33 per cent of the initial cash was left. This meant that once we had Rs 66 lakh left and the investor felt it was not working out, he had the option of just shutting down the company and taking the remaining money. There was also the 1 per cent he had quoted for his involvement in the company to provide management guidance.

As the shareholder documentation was taking time and the investor had confirmed he would be putting in the money, we set up a pseudo board meeting in which we discussed the way ahead. At this meeting, we decided to go ahead and start hiring. Hiring takes time and we didn't want to wait for money in the bank. The investor helped us in that too—he referred a few people to CoCubes. This was the time our friend Sachin also came on board. He became the owner of 7 per cent equity in CoCubes. He was working in Mumbai; both he and his wife left their jobs so that Sachin could move to CoCubes in Gurgaon. We were now twelve-people-strong.

But by the beginning of July we didn't have money to even pay our electricity bill. As Aman was reinvesting in this round, we reached out to him to ask for an advance on the upcoming investment. We were all sure that the investment would happen, so Aman wired us Rs 2 lakh to help take care of the expenses.

Then the investor went on a trip to the US for two weeks. By the time he returned, something had flipped. He wrote us an email on 24 July 2008, saying: *We need to talk . . . Can you meet me tomorrow in Delhi?* That didn't sound good. When we met, he mentioned that the business didn't seem scaleable to him and that he believed we would need a lot more mentorship and leadership guidance than he had envisioned. He suggested that we reserve enough equity (around 15 per cent more) for that. He asked us to re-pitch to all the investors so that they could take a call. We were worried now—we had no money in the bank. Sachin and a few other hires had joined and there were more who had resigned.

The investor's final answer ended up being a 'no' for equity investment. We were upfront about our situation and requested the investor for a loan to help tide us over this period. We got an email back saying that that was possible, but if the loan was not paid back in one year's time, with significant interest, it would convert into the investor getting 66 per cent of the common equity. In addition, it had a clause stating that we couldn't raise capital without getting a sign-off from him. One of the senior entrepreneurs we were taking advice from said: 'He is trying to f*** you. You should politely say no and never do business with him again. Start using your own network to raise funds.'

I do think that because we were raising money for the first time, every clause in the term sheet and SHA had seemed onerous to us. Every clause came with permissions that we would need to run our own company, and we took too long to understand and ensure that we were safe on all counts. We had also spent far too much time in arguing about things that were more or less standard. Most importantly, we should never have assumed that the deal was done until the money was in the bank. This is something that I keep telling all founders who are raising their seed round. Make your plans, but don't end up committing to future investments based on a verbal agreement. Wait for the money to hit the bank.

Another lesson we learnt was to really start thinking from the investor's point of view. We all say it, but practising it under pressure takes a calm mind. When we were pushed against the wall, our argument to the investor was that he should make the investment because he had committed to it; because if he didn't, we would be screwed. This is not a rational argument. The only argument that needs to be made should focus on why investing would make the investor a lot of money.

The next few months were difficult. We borrowed a couple of lakhs from our parents to keep CoCubes afloat. We had to let go of some folks we had recently hired. This was the first time we were asking someone to leave because of company performance. It was hard, but it had to be done. Trilegal had helped us with the term sheet and SHA but now we had no money to pay them. We had incurred a bill of Rs 2.72 lakh while negotiating the deal. So I called the partner at Trilegal and said that while we didn't have the money to pay them at the moment, we did intend to pay fully. We offered them equity in the company. Trilegal said (and rightly so) that taking equity was not their firm's policy. But they agreed to wait for their fees and didn't charge us any interest.

I think it would have been easy for them to play hardball and squeeze us dry. Instead, they behaved extremely graciously.

These are the acts of kindness that one remembers after so many years.

Things hadn't gone according to plan but during the seed round we had managed to avoid a few things. One of them was not to use our credit cards to fund the company. Another was to not take too much money from our parents (if you belong to the middle class like us). Parents in India don't refuse their kids, and it is easy to bank on them because you believe it will work. But one can never guarantee the outcome, so it is best to find someone outside the family who believes in the idea as much as you do and wants to genuinely invest in you. Family should never be taken for granted.

Also, we had been wary of people who didn't want to invest money but wanted equity in return for any help. I regularly meet first-time entrepreneurs who get offers from individuals who say they can't invest money, but for some percentage of equity they would be willing to help them with sales and making connections. These individuals have a lot of experience in the industry, are extremely polished and exude confidence. My advice here has been to always ask for money from them. If a person is unwilling to invest his money in your start-up, it means he doesn't believe in it enough to hold any equity.

To keep the company running I had to borrow Rs 2 lakh from my then girlfriend and now wife, Bhakti (who was working in London at the time). This was all the spare cash she had. Meanwhile, Aman introduced us to his batchmate Rajiv Raghunandan (who currently runs Arali Ventures), who pulled in his colleague Nikesh Shah. By the end of November 2008, we had raised Rs 10 lakh from them at a valuation of Rs 5 crore. It took only one meeting for them to trust us and put in the money. The only onerous clause in the agreement was that if we didn't attain revenues of Rs 50 lakh in eighteen months, the stake of the investors would double. Aman, too, converted the 2 lakh he had sent in anticipation of earlier rounds to equity. We now had money for four to six months in the bank and could focus on raising venture capital.

six

raising the vc round

We formally rejected the offer of taking the loan from our angel investor on 11 August 2008, and with it ended our 'no-shop agreement' of not talking to other investors while these discussions were in progress.

The following day, I took the help of our senior from college, Kashyap Deorah, who sent the following email to Raghu Batta at Ojas Ventures.

Raghu and Harpreet, please meet each other.

Raghu:
Harpreet and Vibhore, both IIT-B grads, have a company called CoCubes. I've known Harpreet since 2003, when he was the publicity manager of Techfest; and I am a fan of his undying energy, high resilience as an entrepreneur and good business acumen. I've closely seen him build CoCubes from scratch, and I

think his team has built a very cool placement tool for engineering college students to connect with employers. I personally believe that the best Indian social networks will be around higher education, than around media and entertainment. CoCubes falls in just that bucket where the benefits of social networking are applied to the must-have needs of a large Indian community. They are fairly at an early stage but already have revenues and a solid team. They have an early-stage investor and are now looking for VC money to scale the business.

Harpreet: We have already spoken about Raghu.
I hope you two will connect directly and benefit from this connection.

Best,
Kashyap

A lot of entrepreneurs ask for introductions to venture capitalists, and the email above is just the kind of introduction one should look for because:

- *It comes from a trusted source*: Kashyap had already built and sold a company while he was in college. When he sent this email, he was already running his second start-up.
- *It states why the VC should be interested*: Kashyap mentioned in detail why he thought Harpreet was a good founder and why CoCubes was a good deal for Ojas to consider. The strength of an introduction goes a long way in building trust, because, in the end, getting money from an investor is about the investor having enough trust in you to put their cash into your pocket.

The environment in 2008 was different as compared to today. Data information platform Crunchbase today lists about 138 organizations in India doing early-stage investments. In 2008, there were no more than six early-stage venture capital firms in the country—Accel, Ojas, Helion, Footprint, Indavest and Seedfund. Sequoia and Matrix were there as well but were mostly into growth-stage investing.

Nowadays, when you start pitching your start-up, a good strategy is to approach the venture capital funds that are the lowest priority for you. By the time you get to the ones you really want on your shareholder table, your pitch will have improved. In 2008, this was not an option because there were not enough funds to exhaust.

Along with Ojas, we were also introduced to the other venture capital guys, but it didn't work out. We also got connected to Alok Mittal, who was running Canaan Partners at the time and was also an angel investor. But he'd offered a valuation of Rs 2.5 crore, which we were not willing to take up.

With Ojas, it took time and a couple of follow-ups to schedule the first call. It happened a couple of weeks after the introduction. This, too, has changed in recent times. As the number of venture capitalists has increased, the competition among them to invest in the best deals has also intensified, which has subsequently reduced the time they take to get back to you.

The last six months of to and fro with the angel investor had taught us a lot. We understood the standard deal terms, we understood answers to key questions that were important for an investor and we had thought through the business model in detail.

Initially, we had been introduced to Raghu by Kashyap, but now both Raghu and Gautam Balijepalli from Ojas were involved in the discussion. While Raghu had been a venture capitalist in Silicon Valley before moving to India to join Ojas, Gautam had been an associate at Nomura Private Equity. In addition to the questions they had for us, we curated a list of queries posed by our earlier angel investor and other venture capitalists and circulated that with our answers. By this time, we had figured out that we knew the market better than most venture capitalists, and it was important to share that knowledge. For several questions, such as *Who are your competitors?*, we now had detailed notes along with a deck on our competitors' strengths and weaknesses. By the time October 2008 came to an end, we had weathered the initial hiccups with Ojas. Gautam wrote that he wanted to talk to some of our customers. Overall, in our conversation with Ojas, we kept our responses prompt and to the point. We readily accepted what we didn't know and learnt a lot in the process. Where we needed advice, we wrote to Raghu and Gautam and engaged in a conversation. In those early days, there was always confusion about who was the best person to approach in a large company while selling the CoCubes solution. Was it the HR head or the CEO? This was important from a hiring perspective for us as well, because a person who speaks to CEOs is different from a person required to talk to the HR head, who in turn is different from a person required to talk to campus heads. We would bounce around topics like these with Gautam and Raghu. This helped us build a relationship and set the tone for working together. In general, there is so much happening in a start-up that you have a lot to share, which can have a positive influence on the venture capitalist who is evaluating you. We shared ideas constantly.

We set up Google alerts to find news related to what we were building at CoCubes and kept communicating with Ojas. We would share any news item on the topic of Indian universities lacking placement services or students in tier-2 colleges not getting jobs. I would go to a client meeting and, only if it had gone well, share notes from the meeting with Ojas. Then, as sales with that client progressed, I would keep sharing the updates. There were still periods of silence from their side, and we had to find creative ways to break that silence through emails that could pique interest without seeming intrusive. Irrespective of whether an angel or venture capitalist invests or not, one of the best outcomes of interacting with them is getting introduced to the relevant people. To evaluate a company in detail, they introduce you to prospective customers or senior people in the industry, people you would normally not have access to as a first-time entrepreneur. I loved that part because it was helping our business directly, and we made sure we did well in all those meetings. All this time Vibhore, myself and our team were working day and night, to the point that Gautam wrote us the email below.

From: Gautam Balijepalli
Sent: Thursday, 4 December 2008
To: Harpreet S. Grover
Cc: Vibhore Goyal
Subject: *Quick question*

When do you guys sleep? :)

The most difficult hurdle we had to overcome during the fundraising was something we could not have foreseen. Our idea was unique, and we had believed that having a unique idea was a positive. Turns out it wasn't. There was no one in the US or Europe doing what we were; there was no one else in India who was doing it at that time either. A unique idea scares venture capitalists. The rationale is that if this idea is as good as the entrepreneur believes it to be, why aren't other folks doing it? It is much easier for a venture capitalist to be convinced about funding you if a similar idea has been funded abroad, or by another VC fund locally.

Thankfully, around that time, Naukri.com launched Firstnaukri.com. This helped provide evidence to Ojas that large companies were thinking of the same problem that we were: helping students land their first job. The general rule is that if a large company is investing time and energy in doing something, it must be a large-enough market size. Meanwhile, I also set up a meeting with the person who was heading Firstnaukri. During the meeting, I shared more about what we were doing and also understood what the internal dynamics at their end were. Armed with more information, we went back to Ojas and argued why we thought CoCubes would win over Firstnaukri.com. But it was interesting to realize that being unique is not great and that those ideas have a harder time raising capital—and generally fail the first time around.

By November 2008, we had been chatting for four months and had exchanged 128 emails providing information, exchanging thoughts, and educating both ourselves and our venture capitalists. But a company can't run on knowledge alone. It needs money. So we decided to email Ojas, wanting to know if they would like to give us a term sheet. This had the desired effect and we got our first investment committee meeting, resulting in a term sheet on 15 December to raise Rs 3.5 crore at a post-money valuation of Rs 10.5 crore.[1]

By now, I was freely asking Gautam for references in the industry and sharing information about my friends who had just started companies and were looking to raise money. Amongst many others, I introduced them to Rohit Bansal, the founder of Snapdeal, who, along with Kunal Bahl, was looking to raise their first round of funding—Ojas passed the deal!

This time around, we understood the term sheet clauses well and knew what to fight and what not to. We didn't engage a lawyer this time and took help from other entrepreneurs to think it through. We signed the SHA at the end of February 2009, with money hitting the bank on 25 March. After celebrating with our team, Vibhore and I got a bottle of champagne, sat at a roadside dhaba and celebrated with the bubbly, dal tadka and roti. We finally had the ammunition to start building the company we had dreamed of.

seven

we work 24/7

How many days a week do you work?

We were asked this question by a lot of people interviewing for positions at CoCubes. Our answer: *We work 24/7*. We wanted there to be no ambiguity on what to expect once a person joined the company. We were open to the person growing fast, but we wanted folks who were willing to give every single day to CoCubes.

Pursuant to closing the investment round, we went into overdrive. We wanted to sign up more colleges and companies and hire a lot of people. One of the first things that happens after a funding round is a board meeting. In March 2009, we didn't have the space to conduct the board meeting at our office. We still believed that we should save every penny and ended up having the meeting at our house. We projected the presentation on the wall and placed our dining-table chairs around it. Below the projected deck, the plaster on the wall was coming off due to seepage. At the end of the day, Raghu said, 'I understand your need for frugality, but it will be best if we rent a place for a day to do our board meetings. Or you fly to Bangalore to do them at the Ojas office.'

At the end of the meeting, we set ourselves a target of signing on 100 companies and 1000 colleges by December 2010, an eighteen-month time frame. But once we got on the ground, there were so many things to think through: What was the reason for large companies to buy from us? How did it differ for medium- and small-size firms? Should we build the product for both large and small companies? How to attract companies in different sectors? How to move beyond engineering colleges? How to target students directly?

This happens to the simplest of ideas. The number of threads one can pursue are endless, and it is the role of the founders to ensure that the company picks and sticks to the thread that leads to maximum value creation in the long term.

Hiring after Funding

By now, one and a half years into running CoCubes, we had enough traction in colleges to try and hire a college sales head. Like most other entrepreneurs, my first hunch was to hire someone who was experienced enough, already knew the colleges and who had managed a team before. People of this description are generally found in large companies. I reached out to someone who was heading the campus team for a large BPO company. He had earlier been an entrepreneur too, and after running his family business for some time, had joined a large corporate. We convinced him to join us. We gave him a pay hike of more than 50 per cent. Also, his existing firm was paying for his executive MBA, so we agreed to pay his company back for the same. I remember fighting with Vibhore to justify this hire, saying: *Look at the risk the person is taking with his career. And we need this person, he has college contacts.* I remember being excited at the prospect of someone from a brand joining our small company and saw it as a big victory. But my joy was short-lived.

In a large company, there is a travel desk to book your tickets, a cafeteria for food, the hotels you stay in are nice. And most often the respect a third party (in our case, colleges) has is not for the individual but for the *position* the individual enjoys in a large company. Armed with the visiting card of a large company, one can procure a meeting easily. This doesn't happen when you work with a start-up. In a large company, because a lot is already set up and running, the work to do is mostly fine-tuning, as opposed to being in a start-up, which needs you to build everything from scratch. Also, we realized that the knowledge of understanding the college market was far less important than the skill it took to build and lead a team. We had hired someone who would be the fastest off the block, when, instead, we should have hired for the long term. Also, during the interview process, as a young CEO looking to hire someone senior for the first time, I had not asked the truly difficult questions about the role because I was afraid of putting the candidate off.

By the beginning of 2010, it was clear that the hired leader wasn't the right one. I realized that I personally didn't want to go and sell to colleges. The college market didn't suit my strengths. And I hated that the selling in colleges wasn't professional enough—it is possible that one would have to wait for a long time to meet the concerned parties, to get money in the bank might need multiple calls to the owner, and so on. Also, most colleges were located in tier-2 towns, which meant constant travel, making it difficult to manage other stuff at the company. So we decided to look for someone who could lead the entire college vertical; not only a sales head but a person who could evolve into a business head.

This time around, I decided to go with a reference. I asked around, but very few IITians wanted to be in sales. Most were doing analytics, consulting, operations and research—there was almost no one in sales. The only person I knew a little was Sameer Nagpal. He was from IIT Kanpur and was a friend of my former flatmate, Mrutyunjaya Panda. I had met him once when was visiting Panda. I called Panda to ask, 'How is the guy? We need to hire for sales.' Panda said Sameer loved to do sales and that once he thinks of getting something done, he does it. So I wrote to Sameer.

At the time, Sameer was leading sales for a multinational company in Pune. I wasn't thrilled to know that he was at a large company, but when I spoke to him, I realized that he also didn't like being in one. He didn't like that sales incentives were capped and processes did not encourage collaboration between teams. We decided to meet and Sameer flew in to see us at our office at the Ansal Institute of Technology. We spent a full day together. He met Vibhore and our other teammates. It was a good meeting and I was feeling positive about taking the next steps.

Then, as I was walking him out, I asked him where his parents lived. He said Delhi. I asked him if he was meeting them. He said no, as he hadn't told them he would be in town, and joked about how sometimes he had coincidentally run into his surprised mother at the airport. I was a little taken aback by this and rethought our decision. I wanted to check if Sameer was someone who built and valued close relationships. As Sameer made his way to the airport, I called Panda. He assured me that Sameer was a family-oriented person, but I decided to spend more time pondering. I called Sameer to say that I would be in Pune and asked if I could stay at his place. He was open to it. I found out later that this had been his way of evaluating me. He wanted his wife to say yes to this too. We had a great evening together. His wife, Swetha, and I spent time pulling his leg, and well, Sameer ended up joining CoCubes as the head of sales and staying for ten short years.

In general, at CoCubes, we put in a lot of effort in our leadership hiring. When Nilay Kothari joined our technology team, he stayed at Vibhore's house for the first two weeks. Similarly, for the first six months when Sameer was travelling back and forth from Pune (where his wife was working), he used to stay at my place. This helped us get the personal equation right, which set the right foundation for working together.

We were ten people before the funding, with our friend Sachin (who had joined before the failed angel funding round) being the only other senior leader apart from Vibhore and myself. By early 2010, we had expanded to thirty-four, with four senior leaders. The company had fanned out into different functions; corporate sales, college sales, operations and technology were the major pillars.

Most of the initial hires came from two sources: references or campus hiring. This was the time when the Indian economy was in a depression and, as a result, campus hiring had slowed down considerably. So as a start-up offering reasonable starting salaries, we were able to get great-quality candidates.

Nobody tells a first-time entrepreneur how hiring is such a big part of running a company. Attracting the right people to work in your company is a full-time job. We made a lot of mistakes in hiring, but, over time, came up with these golden rules for hiring people for different levels:

- At the entry level, we hired people who had demonstrated doing any one thing well and had a positive attitude to learn. So someone could be a state player in cricket, a black belt in karate or an artist from the National School of Drama. This proved to us that the person, at some point in his or her life, had shown persistence to do one thing properly. The hope was that if the person has been able to do one thing well out of their own interest, then, if sufficiently excited, they would be able to do this job well too.

- For mid-level hiring, we realized that with a few years of experience, people learn the art of giving the right answers. They say what you want to hear, hence interviewing them is less useful. In such cases, the thing that we hinged our decisions on was a detailed reference check from their previous employers.

- In our leadership hires, we made a lot of mistakes, but we did eventually get it right. Apart from other learnings, we realized that it was important for the families to be on board. Because one ends up spending so much time on the start-up, if the person's family isn't fully supportive and invested as well, it will become difficult for the role to work out. So we would meet their families and they would meet ours, or we would do a double date.

We figured out that the right kind of people for an early-stage start-up with less funding are people with at least one drawback. Generally, the drawback is either 'weak spoken English' or graduation from a 'no-name college'. These are the people ignored by the big companies because they are biased towards certain colleges and types of hires. They want someone polished. That leaves a large pool of fresh graduates who can be employed and trained by start-ups. Many of these folks are naturally hungry to achieve. They want to succeed in life as much as you want to build your start-up.

eight

million-dollar stake

We had signed on our first college for Rs 10,000 as the annual fee. This was a college called Baba Banda Singh Bahadur Engineering College in Fatehgarh Sahib, Punjab. This was a big win for us because someone had trusted us enough to give us actual money. We thought we wouldn't cash the cheque and frame it, but we really needed the money before the venture capital round. On the corporate side, we had signed up with Evalueserve, who gave us Rs 3500 per campus to use our campus-hiring platform.

Overall, we had little idea on how pricing worked in the business-to-business (B2B) sector. There was no comparable product in the market like ours, so looking at others was not an option. I had happened to meet Kartik (co-founder of iTrust and PropTiger) at a conference and requested his time. He invited me to his office for lunch. There I met his co-founder, Dhruv Agarwala. During lunch, Dhruv asked a question which made us look at pricing. He said, 'You charge Rs 10,000 for a college to sign up and Rs 3500 per campus drive. How big is your entire market in India? If I do the math today, the total market size in India works out to be less than 8 million dollars. Why would an investor continue to invest in a company which is working in such a small market?' It was a fair question. As twenty-four-year-olds, we hadn't thought about this deeply enough. We were busy building what we liked building.

So we discussed his question with the team, and we decided to experiment with pricing. We said, let us try and ask more from the customer and see what happens. We had recently hired a salesperson named Amit Das, who used this pricing flexibility and, in his first week at CoCubes, closed on a deal with a college for Rs 25,000. Then, in a month, he was able to close another deal for Rs 35,000. This gave us confidence. Over the next couple of years, we kept experimenting with pricing. We realized that charging companies for the platform for campus hiring was a small software-as-a-service (SaaS) market, so we stopped charging for that service. This led to more companies signing up, which we used to increase our pricing for colleges. By 2011, our average college deal size was more than Rs 2 lakh. This was significantly better than the pricing that we had started with two years ago.

We also kept adding services for the colleges. We partnered with India's leading assessment company to help students benchmark themselves. We embedded English-learning software so that employability could improve. We shot videos of candidates so that companies could gauge their soft skills. We had started off as a company that collected the database from colleges and made it visible online. But we identified a lot of other problems in the ecosystem and realized there was a larger play possible—where we could also test students in colleges.

On the corporate side, the recession blues were beginning to fade. IT companies had started hiring in thousands again. But most of them gave offers in advance and students had to wait a year before joining. So we built a product to help companies stay engaged with the hired candidates. Over time, we tweaked our product to help companies start engaging with candidates in their pre-final year of college. This was called 'engagement pages'. Corporates could now put out updates and students from different colleges could follow. This was closer to the dream that we wanted to build—that any student from any college in the country could follow his or her dream company. Cognizant, Accenture, CMC, Yes Bank, Capgemini and a lot of other companies signed up. They started paying us Rs 5 lakh per year to get on to this platform. We had stopped charging companies earlier. This was a significant win for us, and as founders we were excited about the direction the company was taking.

One thing we did well was to keep the college and corporate teams separate. We wanted to do this because of the amount of corruption we'd heard about in the college market—that colleges regularly paid HRs in companies to visit their campus. By keeping the teams separate, we ensured that there was no person in the company who knew both the demand and the supply side. This reduced our risk of anyone bypassing the CoCubes platform and taking a client company directly to the college in exchange for money.

Positive Signs for CoCubes

Our revenue in the first year after funding, in 2009–10, went from Rs 6 lakh per annum to Rs 35 lakh per annum. In 2010–11, it went up to Rs 2 crore. We started making plans to hit the Rs 10-crore mark soon. But we were also running out of money and decided to go to the market again to raise more capital for funding this growth. Overall, the conversations were positive, but the size of the college market still seemed to be a concern. Ojas was bullish on CoCubes and offered a million dollars more to continue building the company before we raised the next round. We did that round at a valuation of Rs 35 crore post-money. By now, our model seemed to have matured and our valuation had jumped four times in eighteen months. As young founders, for the first time, the value of our stake became greater than a million dollars each.

We were in the news quite a lot, and that too without spending a rupee. Our only effort was hiring two young fellows named Deepak Chawla and Anand Subramanian who had an interest in marketing. They made a list of all the awards out there and ensured that we put in our entries for all of them. This turned out to be one of the best investments of time and energy. CoCubes was featured on business and finance news channel ET Now; we won the NASSCOM Emerge 50 award for emerging companies, among other awards, and we also won the TiE-Lumis award for the best upcoming start-up in the country.

As our belief in the idea grew, and now that we had money again from Ojas to last us eighteen months, there was a major development. We approached Aman (our first angel investor) to join CoCubes full-time. He had been involved with CoCubes from day zero, as the first backer, and had supported us through our journey, from working with us on the first business plan to helping us understand what complex terms like EBITDA meant. He had left Inductis and moved to Bangalore for a new role where he was managing a P&L of 10 million dollars and a team of more than 150 people. Our pitch to him was to come on board as the president of the company and take ownership of sales and operations. We thought that we had now derived the right formula and that an experienced person like Aman would help us translate it into a viable business.

Sameer and I went to Aman's house. We spent the evening taking his inputs on revising our legal contracts with colleges. By the morning we had rolled out the new contracts to our sales team and set up a training process. Aman loved this. He had been in the corporate field for a long time, where things moved slowly. He also loved the feel of ideas converting into action at a fast pace. The conversation went well. I remember Vibhore and I being on a call with him, offering him a 5 per cent stake in CoCubes, while he was asking for 10 per cent. In a matter of five minutes we had ended the call and closed on 7 per cent. Aman agreed to bear a 50 per cent cut in fixed salary and move his entire family back to Gurgaon.

Over the last year, our team size had also grown. We were eighteen people when we had taken funding. By the end of 2010, we were closer to seventy, and it was a tight fit in our small office space at the Ansal Institute. Also, our original benefactors, Dr Singh and Dr Yadav, had left the institute. We were called to meet the new director, who believed that equity had no value. She wanted Rs 2 lakh to be paid to the institute in lieu of the equity. We tried persuading her to hold on to the equity, but she didn't budge.

As the new funding from Ojas came in, one of the first things we did was to sign on for a new office space. The process had obviously started before the money came in, and company resources had been directed towards it. We were also looking to hire aggressively. Our Excel sheet showed us that we would grow to over 100 employees in the following year. While thirty of these would be sales folks, the rest would be people sitting in the office. We would also need a room to conduct frequent training sessions. To make it a little interesting, we raised the height of each row in the training room so that it looked like an auditorium. A boardroom was necessary now that the leadership team was bigger, and we needed a place to discuss and plan things. We also had this vision of an 'ideas room', where all the walls would basically be a whiteboard, including the door. With colourful markers strewn around, it would be the place for us to think alone or brainstorm with colleagues. We thought there should be about 100 seats in the office because we didn't want to move if we hired more people as the business grew and we raised more money.

We ended up getting a customized 8000 sq. ft office space in a nice building in Gurgaon. Aman negotiated hard on the rent and got a good deal with a two-year lock-in. That was good with us because we were here to stay.

We had kept the rent in check for the first four years of the company. We had paid a total of less than Rs 6 lakh in those four years, also factoring in the rent for the apartment we lived in. The office we had within the college was procured in exchange for equity shares in CoCubes. From those fairly humble beginnings, we went up to paying Rs 4.5 lakh every month in 2011, with Rs 30 lakh as the security deposit.

As we moved into the new office, we were grateful for where we had reached. We sent a letter to the parents of all the team members working at CoCubes, thanking them for sharing their offspring with us and partaking in our vision. Our parents and friends came in to visit, clicking pictures and posting them online. Six years out of IIT, we had a fancy, colourful office, venture capital funds and a vision to fulfil.

1 July 2011 rolled around and, sitting in our new office, all of us felt geared up for the bigger things we could see coming our way.

# of friendships lost and found

'Never ever contact me again!' Those were the last words I heard from Sachin in September 2010.

In Patiala, our family used to live in the corner house. Four houses away, in the lane next to ours, was Sachin's house. My parents had shifted to Patiala from Delhi when I was in class four. From then until the time I went to IIT, Sachin and I would play cricket together—every evening without fail. On the weekends, hours would pass by with a bat and ball. Sometimes other friends joined in, but even if they didn't, we would play all day long. Sachin was a couple of years older than me. By the time he joined college in Patiala after class twelve, I was just getting serious about preparing for IIT. While the cricket playing lessened, we always found time in the evening to go and drink chicken soup from a roadside stall close by.

Once I moved to IIT Bombay, our interaction became infrequent for a couple of years. There were no mobile phones, and the only way to interact was through landlines. Both of us got busy, till one day, when I got a call on the common landline in Hostel 5. Sachin had got a job in Mumbai and was moving here. He had graduated with some other degree in hand but was good at programming. His job and house were both close to IIT, and we started meeting again regularly. We were both keen on fitness and enjoyed going to the gym together. We would spend hours talking to each other about our families, love affairs, dreams and hopes.

We had now known each other for more than ten years and could guess what the other person had to say before they said it. I was more objective while Sachin was more emotional. Vibhore was my room-mate and close friend, but in Sachin I had a brother. Our families knew how close we were and, often, two boxes of home-made sweets would be sent over after the holidays—one for all the friends in IIT and one for the brother.

In our batch, there were 420 boys and twenty-one girls, so finding a girlfriend within IIT was, to put it simply, beyond my abilities. In the fourth year, when Sachin called me and said, '*Oye*, my manager has assigned me to help two girls from a local college in their internship,' I picked up my bike and rushed to the spot. And there they were, Meena and Bhakti, two girls who had popped out of nowhere. And it worked out. Two best friends marrying two best friends.

Sachin continued doing well in his job in Mumbai. He had also got to know Vibhore well during that time and we used to hang out a lot together. So when Vibhore and I started a company, it was understood that it was a matter of time before Sachin joined us. The only issue was convincing his dad that leaving a steady job to join a start-up with his friends was a good idea. His father didn't like the idea of start-ups. But Sachin finally took the plunge, moving from Mumbai to Gurgaon in 2008. He had married Meena by then and she had also left her job to look for one in Gurgaon. Just before Sachin was about to join, our funding round got pulled. Vibhore and I called to inform him that paying salaries would be tough. But he said that he had already decided to join and took a 90 per cent cut till the time we could get another round of funds. He had 7 per cent equity in CoCubes. His father cautioned him, saying, 'Beta, you will be the third person in the start-up, they are already a pair. You will be singled out.' Sachin had laughed it away. After all, we were brothers.

Sachin joined and started working with Vibhore. Along with Vibhore and myself, he became the third pillar at CoCubes. We would work all day and night. There were no other thoughts in our heads except to make CoCubes stronger. The schedule was hectic. It was almost a year before the cracks started appearing. Vibhore and Sachin's working styles were very different, so ingrained in each of them, that it was becoming hard to reconcile the two, even though they both had the same goal—to make CoCubes successful.

There were many times when I got pulled in to ensure peace.

Two years after Sachin had joined CoCubes, it came to a point where both Sachin and Vibhore announced to me that they couldn't work with each other any more. This meant one of them had to go.

I said to Vibhore, 'Let me speak to Sachin.' But I couldn't look him in the eye. He, too, knew it wasn't working out. That's when he told me to never contact him again and walked away.

Bhakti cried when I told her about this. Sachin was her rakhi brother, Meena was her best friend, and Bhakti didn't know if they would to talk to her any more. We had to break the news to the team. It was hard to explain why Sachin had left in a hurry, why the relationship was so strained with someone who was brought in as a senior person and best friend.

We spoke to our board. Given that the company was doing well, Ojas was okay to buy all of Sachin's ESOP at the price of the last round. That got done quickly. Sachin, meanwhile, blocked my number. He continued to stay in Gurgaon. I tried reaching out over text a couple of times—he never responded. I knew where he lived. On so many days I thought of stopping by his house and knocking on his door. But I didn't have the courage to face him. Bhakti visited them sometimes and I would keep getting some bits of information from her. But Sachin and I did not meet for six long years. During these years, he had a daughter, I had a daughter, CoCubes went through hell and got back on its feet. And life kept going on.

Fate intervened in January 2016. I had become serious about fitness and had set out to run the Airtel Delhi Half-Marathon. As soon as I finished, I spotted Sachin in the sea of runners. Almost at the same time, he spotted me. He turned his back to me and started walking away. I rushed after him, calling his name. He didn't look back.

I caught up with him, put a hand on his shoulder and the words 'I am sorry' tumbled out of my mouth. That is what I felt for all the years we'd lost. He turned around and said, '*Yaar, itne saal lagg gaye to say I am sorry. Pehle hi bol diya hota* [Bro, it took you so long to say I am sorry. You should have just said it sooner].'

We hugged and cried, tears of joy flowing down our cheeks.

At this point, in 2016, after a long time, it felt like everything was going to be all right.

ten

up and . . .

While writing this book, I wrote to Aman to ask him what he had felt during his time at the company. He sent me the following note:

When I joined, one of the first things that struck me was how 'enthusiastic' and 'bold' we were in our ambitions. I vividly recall an instance: We would use Microsoft technology everywhere. Bill Gates was visiting India at that time on an official trip. I could not believe it when I heard a serious discussion in the office on how we could get Bill Gates to visit our premises. People were full of raw energy and bold visions for our future. Even though a lot of times I felt it was far removed from reality, just seeing the energy in the office was infectious.

The other thing that I observed in the initial days was that we all really liked each other. The teams would spend a lot of time together (outside of office hours), would celebrate each other's successes, would cover each other's backs. It was very impressive to see that kind of camaraderie in the organization.

However, coming from a large corporate, the whole environment seemed like the Wild, Wild West.

Sales: *Sales teams were small and not disciplined in executing the processes. Sales folks would commit to meeting a set of people during a week and then go on to meet a completely different set of people who were not even on the calling list.*

Operations: *Our operations were complex. The fact that several elements of the processes were manual and not automated did not help. This resulted in a lack of accountability and poor customer experience. The operations teams were always 'huffing and puffing', trying to douse one fire after another.*

Finance: *This was a serious headache for us. Our invoices were not raised on time and our credit cycles would run into four to six months. We did not have appropriate financial reporting in place. As we started scaling up, given the poor collections and poor cost discipline, our cash was getting guzzled fast.*

~

Bringing Aman in brought about a lot of discipline across functions and teams. Over the next two years, most of his time went in bringing about discipline, making the teams sensitive to costs while leading the entire sales and operations process. The teams responded well to the measures he put in place.

These were things that would help CoCubes go a long way. Personally, it set the base for a lot of learning for me, helping me to see how good execution was important to making your vision a reality.

In our enthusiasm to streamline processes we also overdid some things. We started creating detailed process maps and spent a lot of energy on them. But we were growing so fast that by the time we rolled out a process, it had already been changed or improved. Additionally, we created a lot of trackers, which increased the workload overall. Now, the person had to do the actual work and update the tracker—something I, too, had hated at Inductis (and I still don't know of anybody who loves it).

Busy Days

In 2011–12, our goal for the company was to achieve Rs 10 crore in revenue. Almost 80 per cent of this revenue was expected to come from colleges. This target was broken down into regions and given to the salespeople. There were protests from some quarters that these numbers were not achievable, but in the euphoria that had taken over us, these arguments were easily resolved and dealt with. By now, we had evolved the college model and were offering a complete employability-enhancement module to students.

Our engagement pages for companies were the highlight. Companies used these pages to stay in touch with students from different colleges. In 2011, our largest clients had 100,000+ followers, and if you googled the company name, our engagement page would appear in the top five links. To address this demand, we launched more engagement features.

But the list of requests from clients was endless. This was the first time they had seen something like this and, now, they were asking for the moon. There was a downside to this model, though. Getting content from the companies was difficult. It had to go through layers of marketing approvals, and when it finally came out, it was boring. The students were mostly interested in asking how they could get a job with the company.

As updates to products slowed down, the discussions between Vibhore and myself occasionally became a little heated. He felt that we now had too many modules to manage for the technical team, whose size hadn't grown so much. We were trying to serve companies, colleges and students all at the same time. All of these pulled our limited tech resources in multiple directions, as each direction contributed a bit to the overall revenue. If we could go back, one of the things we would do as founders is to look at what was really working, focus on that and stop spending time and resources on the rest. Place a bet and back it with conviction.

In December 2011, we collected Rs 1 crore from clients in one month. This was big for us. Given that we had moved to a point where we were charging Rs 700 per student, the market size had increased dramatically on paper. By March 2012, the company had grown to eighty-six people. And we were still hiring. We had about Rs 6 crore in the bank and were on track towards our 10-crore annual-revenue goal.

Acquiring sQuotient

It was around this time that we realized that connecting colleges and companies was not enough. Even if we connected both of them, the hiring ratios were so bad that both the candidates and the companies remained unhappy. This was because of the lack of employability among students in college. We built our own assessment platform which companies could use to hire quality candidates. We offered this to corporates for free and they used our platform to upload content and run assessments.

As we interacted with clients, we saw that many corporates didn't have the content to run assessments—and we didn't have the in-house expertise to build it. One of the transitions that was still happening at the time was the moving of assessments from offline to online platforms. For the last ten years, large firms like Infosys had been conducting assessments offline. Papers were printed and transported across the country to different venues and distributed to students. Then an OMR (optical mark recognition) machine would be used to check them. But this was changing.

I met the founder of one of the larger assessment companies and he told me that doing assessments online wasn't possible as colleges didn't have enough computer systems. I knew from our recent experience in colleges that this wasn't true. I realized that day that the advice of experts should be taken with a pinch of salt. Several times they just refer to an old reality while the world has moved on.

Online assessment was an opportunity, but we needed the expertise to do it. The best way to go about this was through an acquisition. Over the last few years I had sporadically been in touch with Saurabh Misra. He was the founder of sQuotient, and they were doing over 100,000 assessments annually for customers like Microsoft and Mu-Sigma, among others. But most of their assessment work was offline. They worked out of Science and Technology Entrepreneurs Park (STEP) in Noida. I had first met Saurabh at a TiE event in 2008, where we had chatted and agreed to disagree on our strategy to win this market. For the next few years we kept meeting occasionally at some or the other forum, and our affinity for each other kept increasing.

In 2011, the conversation took a serious turn and Vibhore and I met Saurabh to share our vision. We wanted to create an equal opportunity for each candidate, and making assessments free was an important aspect of it. We believed free assessments would accelerate adoption by corporates.

Saurabh and his team had spent years building a company that was making money by selling assessments, and we wanted to make it free. They considered the prospect preposterous but were excited by it too. After a few meetings (which included Saurabh inviting me to his house for a gathering of poetry aficionados so his wife could evaluate me—I seem to have been evaluated by a number of wives beside my own), we agreed to move forward. We hired a law firm in Bangalore to conduct a due diligence on sQuotient. The legal team spent a few days at the sQuotient office, going over all the numbers, and gave us the go-ahead. We bought sQuotient at three times their revenues, paying 25 per cent of the money upfront, with the rest paid up over the next eleven months. Saurabh and his team moved over to the CoCubes office.

Debt and a Term Sheet

Our 2012 revenue booking target was Rs 20 crore. 'Revenue booking' is different from 'serviced revenue'. While the former is the total revenue that the salesperson has been able to sign with the customer, serviced revenue is the amount from the total booked revenue which will be delivered to the customer within the financial year.

Out of Rs 10 crore of the total revenue booking in 2011–12, only Rs 4 crore was revenue serviced in the same year. The rest of it were long-term contracts to be serviced over the next two years. Our cash collection also stood at around Rs 4 crore while we were spending close to Rs 9 crore a year. We had been so excited about booking revenues that we had not paid enough attention to cash flows.

This increase in expenditure and the slower-than-anticipated collections had resulted in CoCubes being left with only about two months of cash runway in the bank. And now we were entering the leanest period of our business—the summer months. Colleges were closed and almost no deals happened. Even if some deals took place, the collection of cash from customers would only take place when the colleges reopened and students paid their fees for the next semester.

This would have been a cause for worry but for the fact that there was real interest from investors in CoCubes, particularly from one venture capital investor whose parent fund had a portfolio of over 300 billion dollars. Ojas had introduced us to the investor at the beginning of March 2012 and things had progressed fairly quickly. By April, their managing director had visited the office and spent a day with us. The meeting had gone well and, after speaking to some of our customers, they had gone ahead and given us a term sheet for raising 5 million dollars at a post-money valuation of 20 million dollars. This would leave the founders with 40 per cent equity in the company after the round, which would be worth 8 million dollars. That was a lot of money for two twenty-eight-year-olds. There was interest from two other large venture capital firms, but the valuation being offered was half of what was specified in the term sheet we had. So we didn't engage with them and accepted the term sheet from the aggressive investor.

In the beginning of May 2012, we won the Indian Express Innovation Award, which we shared with the prospective investor.

We wanted to ensure that we kept the business on the right track till the time the funding concluded. This effectively meant that we wanted to avoid any negative word reaching the investor.

But due to lack of collections, we were almost at a point where we were going to run out of money. In our board meeting, we decided to bring in some debt to cover the period between formalizing the term sheet and getting money from the investor. My father, Vibhore's father, Amanjeet and Raghu together put in Rs 2 crore in CoCubes as short-term debt. Raghu, who was on our board of directors, had contributed Rs 1 crore of his personal money to the venture till the time the funding closed.

We were genuinely on a high. In the last couple of years, we had gone from zero revenue to becoming known all over India. We were a real revenue-making company. We had a good team in place and an office where everything looked good. Vibhore and I had been featured as the hottest entrepreneurs in the country by *BusinessWorld*. CoCubes was counted amongst the Deloitte Technology Fast 50 companies in India.

How could anything go wrong?

eleven

. . . down

Around this time, we also won the Lufthansa entrepreneurship award. The event was hosted by Alok Mittal and was telecast live on TV. Aman went to represent CoCubes. The award was a business-class ticket to Europe, along with a two-week course on entrepreneurship at Oxford University. We laughed at it. We didn't need a course at Oxford, we thought, with the overconfidence of two young and eager twenty-five-year-olds. We also used to do a fun thing with all the things that CoCubes won or what our team members got from visiting colleges. We used to hold an auction in the office with all the teammates and sell the items to the highest bidder. With the money collected, we would go out and party. And the same happened with the ticket to Europe too!

The conversation with the fund in general had been good and positive. We were mostly interacting with two folks—the managing director of the fund and the person running the deal. Once or twice, the managing director had mentioned that he thought the deal was too expensive. But he had signed the term sheet, so we were good. And while my interaction with the person running the deal was good early on, the relationship began to slide a bit during the DD phase. This happened mostly because I thought that he was trying to get most of his work for the deal done through me. So, for any internal presentations, he would reach out to us not only for information but also for getting the entire presentation done. That irritated me; it felt like most of the time I was doing his work. And I let him know that.

A couple of years ago, around the time when Raghu had joined our board, we had gone out for lunch with the board. One thing had led to another and Raghu had remarked, 'You might be smart, Harpreet, but it is better to be wise.' When I look back now, I see how right that comment was. I let the person running the deal get on my nerves because I thought he was getting his work done from me. In retrospect, this was a good thing—it meant that CoCubes had the chance to show itself in the best possible light because *we* were making the deck. Today, I realize it would be such a great position to be in, helping the person do his job well and achieving his KRA while, ensuring, at the same time, that CoCubes got what it wanted—5 million dollars.

But I let my ego come in the way.

As the time frame of the deal stretched on, we got a bit worried and pushed the fund harder to share the signed SHA. But the fund seemed to be dilly-dallying. Hearing about CoCubes through awards and news channels, investment bankers had started approaching us to offer services to raise capital. But as we had signed the term sheet, which contained a 'no shop' clause, we couldn't raise money from others. We were stuck. And our money was running out.

A day before Diwali, we received a message from the fund that they were pulling out of the deal. Our monthly expenses were now hovering at about a crore and we had only Rs 24 lakh left in the bank.

We went to Ojas to ask for money to run CoCubes. Our board alone, now, couldn't take a call. So we met Rajesh, who was the managing director of the fund, and asked for Rs 2 crore to get the company through these times. He was curt and clear—Ojas would give Rs 1 crore in a bridge round to CoCubes. A bridge round is a sum of money generally given by the existing investor to help the company tide over hard times. This came at an 18 per cent interest rate, or a 2 per cent discount, month on month, extending to the next round of valuation. The board also wanted to see a plan of how we would utilize these funds over the next few months.

We got on a call with the board members. The original plan was to cut our monthly expenses to Rs 60 lakh from Rs 1 crore. The situation was serious in terms of cash flow, but the belief was that we would get the money somehow. We had already survived two near-death situations without a serious scratch—this time also, something would work out. About 60 per cent of our expenses comprised salaries, 6 per cent was rent and about 13 per cent was reimbursements. Nothing could change without letting go of the team. But we decided to keep the same cost structure till 31 January 2013 and, post that, make further reductions, if required.

CoCubes had grown and now employed over 120 people. The staff knew that we were fundraising, but except our senior team, the rest didn't know that it was not going well.

In November, we took measures to cut costs. We took a hard look at reimbursement policies and made them tighter. We cut money paid per kilometre for fuel expenses, we made approvals compulsory for any flight travel, and a lot more. As founders, we stopped taking our salaries and halted the bonuses of the top leadership. Aman also let go of a part of his salary for the month. As part of buying sQuotient, we were supposed to pay the investors monthly over eleven months. Half of those payments had gone. We went to the sQuotient investors, stating that we were in the middle of fundraising and requested if we could delay the rest of the payments to the following year. One of the investors in sQuotient was a government entity. It was headed by Prof. Raghunandan, who is a big supporter of start-ups. I met him and explained the situation to him, suggesting an alternative structure. But he replied saying that the board had refused to help us and wanted the payments on time.

Another thing we started doing was charging money for our services from corporates. The average charge for assessments by established companies was more than Rs 200 per candidate. When CoCubes began giving online assessments for free, it created a *hulchul*, or buzz, in the market. We had single-handedly brought on the price crash in corporate assessments. Bleeding dry, we now had to charge for our first assessment offering. There was a mini revolt from the corporate sales team, who were used to selling stuff for free. How could they now go and charge customers?

The CA we had brought in to ensure our financials were in place used to charge us over Rs 1 lakh per month. We let him go, moving to another CA who charged Rs 20,000 per month. We took a hard look at the people in the company.

More than anything else, the shame of having to fire the folks we had just hired and sold a dream to was too much. Acknowledging that, suddenly, from being dollar-rich a month ago, we were now staring into a potential abyss where the company could shut down, was not just hard, it was unacceptable.

So we didn't let go of people.

December was upon us. Investors were on leave. Our conversations with VCs slowed down. We had earlier said no to everyone because we had a term sheet. Now, everyone wanted to know what went wrong. Why did the earlier investor refuse? This was the opposite of FOMO (the fear of missing out). And it hit us badly. I remember writing to someone and getting a reply that they would get back to me by the second week of January. We wondered if we would be around then.

By now, it was becoming clearer that we wouldn't be able to raise the investment in time to keep the company running as before. We let go of underperformers. One of the largest expense items that stood out on the monthly table was Aman's salary. Though he had already taken a 50 per cent salary cut to come to CoCubes, it still formed a substantial part of our monthly expense.

At this point, I contemplated if I should quit the company and let Aman take my place. But I didn't want to feel like a quitter. Both Vibhore and I spoke to Aman. He had given his heart and soul to CoCubes over the last two years. But he had financial commitments because of which he needed monthly inflow too; he couldn't bring his salary to zero, and CoCubes didn't have the money. So we agreed to part ways, gradually, over the next three months.

Our last hope was that our sales team would do a great job in the first quarter of the coming year and get us a lot of revenue. By mid-January, it was clear that we wouldn't be able to pull in enough money to take the company to profitability. The only option left was to let go of most of the employees. Delaying that step was costing us money and we were now at the fag end of our lifeline from Ojas as well—there would be no more money coming in from them.

We spoke to all the leads. In our fancy conference room, we went over the list of people one by one, in detail. Choosing one person over another. How do you let go of people after having a written a letter to their parents the previous year, telling them about the company we were building together? Sameer bore the brunt of it. He had convinced a few high-calibre folks to follow him to CoCubes from National Instruments. They were great performers, but as they were from National Instruments and good colleges, they had high salaries. They had to go. Sameer took his commitments seriously and we knew that the situation was troubling him. It upset everyone as we wrote Yes/No and played out the conversations we needed to have in our minds.

On 1 February 2013, we asked our entire team to come together. We didn't have the money to fly in people from other parts of the country. So some of the team members had to join in over the phone. We told the team the truth. It was tearful, but we shared what had happened. That for CoCubes to survive there was no other way but to become a small company again. We were no longer trying to build a billion-dollar company—we were just trying to survive. We didn't ask anyone to leave the premises. People were welcome to stay, they could use the company laptop to search for their next job. We gave everyone a small severance package using some of the money left—this was the least we could do.

The one important thing that we told everyone was that there would be no more job cuts. That whosoever was on the rolls now, their job was secure. I am sure it sounded hollow, but it was important to tell them that we were not thinking of letting go of any more folks.

We were now in a place where, eight years after graduating from IIT, we had not contributed a single rupee to our households. Instead, we had put the hard-earned money of our parents at risk. Neither of us came from wealthy families. My dad had been in the banking sector for thirty years while Vibhore's dad ran a water-meter distribution business in Jaipur. Our mothers were housewives who had dedicated their lives to looking after the families.

As a company, we had come close to death twice before but both times we had pulled our way through. And good things had happened along the way. But this time it seemed like we were too far gone to survive.

twelve

saving our company

We tried to get people placed in other jobs. We offered them the use of our office for as long as they wanted. In the last forty-eight hours, we had made choices on who to keep and who to let go, on the basis of their longevity in the company. We prioritized that over the skill of the person. We tried to spend as much time as we could in the office. The day after the announcement, Sameer came up to me as I was walking out of the door. He said that the person we had chosen to retain in sales in Rajasthan had just put in his papers. He was scared about what had happened and quit. On the other hand, Rohit Kumar, a recent hire, barely two months old in the company, had also been working in sales in Rajasthan. He hadn't had the time to showcase his performance yet and we had asked him to leave. He had heard that the retained person in his department had resigned, so he went to Sameer and said he was willing to join back. Sameer wanted to discuss this. We spoke for a few minutes and called Rohit to chat. Rohit said that he loved his job and wanted to do it. He understood that the company was going through a hard time, but he believed that we would make it. We hired him back.

We had to take care of a few more things. Aman had stayed for two years but we gave him a full four years' worth of ESOPs. This was the only way we could show him our appreciation. We also moved our salary payout cycle from the last date of the month to the first of the next month. Doing this helped us to deposit tax with the government one month later, helping us save cash for another month. For the shareholders of sQuotient, we mentioned that we could not make the payout in eleven months and decided on a revised schedule of twenty-four months.

To our debt holders, we offered an 18 per cent interest rate. And we agreed on finding a way to start paying interest monthly. We called Raghu to apologize for putting his money at risk. He asked us to spend our time on the company and forget about everything else. In the next few years, as we grew, Raghu, the person with the maximum individual money at stake, never once put pressure on us to get it back. He remained calm, approachable and supportive, and never once made us feel that we had been reckless.

We stopped insuring our laptops. The cost of insuring was about Rs 10,000 per laptop, so we just wrote an email to the team requesting them to take better care of the machines.

We still had a couple of months left in the large office. We went to the builder, explaining our situation, and requested if we could get our 30 lakh deposit back. He shooed us away. We decided to stay and used our deposit as rent.

We used this time to search for a smaller office. We finally found it in a slightly rundown building not too far away from our current office. It was a small 700 sq. ft space. Our biggest problem was trying to fit in our forty-odd people in the place, along with a pantry and a meeting room. To make that happen, we had to reduce the width of the workstations. In our earlier office, the workstations had been ergonomically designed. Now their width was such that the laptops barely fit in and one's hands and arms hung in the air. There was no walking space once everyone sat in their chairs. In the last two years, including the deposit, we had spent more than 25 per cent of our raised capital on a fancy office. That would be equivalent to twenty-five years of rent in the smaller space. But water (and money) had already flown under the bridge and there was little we could do except continue to look forward.

We dreaded coming in to office every day. Once there, one could feel everyone looking up to us. It was important that they saw hope in our body language, in our smiles. Every morning, we would tell ourselves that we could do this. That we would come out of this. And this way we would try and build up confidence before walking into the office.

Before letting go of people, Vibhore and I had discussed several things. Our hearts were really in pursuing engagement; we were less interested in building an assessment company. But the direction of engagement meant that no 'real output' was shown to customers instantly, which meant no immediate revenue. So, rather than letting go of 60 per cent of our people, we would have to let go of 90 per cent. Our goal then would be to build the product that every company would use to engage candidates. This was closer to our vision, but it was not reality. If we pursued this path, along with laying off more people, it would also mean that we couldn't be sure of returning the debt of about Rs 2 crore that we had accrued on our books—

indebted to people whose money was not supposed to be at risk in the first place. That wasn't acceptable to us as founders. We had raised venture capital to run the company. We understood that if we lost that money, we would not be able to give the venture capital firm a return. That's the business-model risk of the venture investor. But this is not the model for debt. Debt money is not supposed to be risked.

Once we let go of people, it was easy to see that we should have done it sooner. If we had let go earlier without waiting for experiments to pan out, we wouldn't have had debt on the company books at all, and we could have done anything we wanted to with the company.

We now decided to pursue the model of building a profitable company. And that depended on building an assessment company. This meant reducing our cost to a bare minimum and earning revenue month after month to meet payroll expectations. So our salaries came to zero, the leadership team took a salary cut and we let go of all large expenses (the fancy CA, a large office, travelling in cabs, and so on).

We stopped caring about how many meetings the salespeople did now. We cared about conversion rates. Every meeting meant extra travel cost, so we asked the sales folks to qualify prospects better, to get conversions over the phone. We didn't want three meetings a day because that would mean booking a cab to go there. We wanted the team to take a bus to go to a qualified meeting, spend quality time with that customer and then get a cheque.

We realized the truth about a lot of things that were not working earlier, and we had to fix them now if we wanted to be profitable.

We created an assessment offering on the college side. We had been charging money on the college side for connecting them to corporates, but our renewal rates were less than 30 per cent. That means that if we signed up 100 customers, only thirty wanted to pay us again next year. This wasn't good. So we decided to use assessments on the college side too to create a test for jobs. Just like how sitting for GRE or GMAT helps graduates apply for higher studies, we created a test called PRE-ASSESS for graduates to apply for jobs. That became a hard value proposition we could 'deliver' to the colleges, instead of the promise of taking their students online and making them visible. Earlier, we had scaled up our sales team without finding the product market fit. Now, we had to find the product market fit first.

We also started to charge corporates for assessments. We created a list of each large and small customer we had signed up and filled in numbers on how much value we were adding to them. We then called them to say that from the next month we would charge for our online assessment service. This led to a lot of customers saying no to working with us, but the ones who remained gave us money. And each cheque took us closer to profitability.

We changed all incentives to be paid out on money hitting the CoCubes bank account. Our old incentive structure had been based on 'revenue booking'. This meant the salesperson got paid once he booked revenue. So we had incentivized the sales folks to sign long-term contracts with college customers. However, this was a good thing only if the customer was satisfied and was in fact paying us—which wasn't the case. So the sales folks went home with their incentives and CoCubes was left holding the bag of uncollected cash. An empty bag.

We immediately changed all incentive structures to getting money in the bank. This meant that a salesperson only got incentive for the money that had already come in to the CoCubes bank account.

We replaced processes by trust. We had put in place a lot of processes and Excel files. We junked them and replaced them with trust. That meant that if someone said that they would do something, they did it. There was no need to track the same. We were now back to being about forty people, most of us old-timers. Moving to a smaller office brought us closer— not only in terms of distance but as a team as well; a joke cracked anywhere in the office could be heard on the other side too and the entire office would laugh together. Someone who needed help had to just say it out loud and the helping hands would be ready. In our earlier office, we had place to play cricket inside. We were still playing cricket but outside the office, in the corridor, now. We were no longer strangers at a cocktail party. We were back to being old friends.

Now, the only focus was on cash flow—on getting enough money at the end of the month to pay salaries while we figured out a new path. We caught a break when I met Arun Rao, an old contact. He had earlier founded an assessment company called Origen Test and was now working with TCS iON, which had in no time become the largest assessment company in India.

I met Arun and told him about our plans to turn around the company. He offered us a chance to work with TCS iON. He said that they wanted to create good content for various examinations, and if we were willing to do that, this could mean reasonable money. We immediately picked this up. This was not our core business. The business of selling content adds less value in the long term because you can only use the created question once to sell. You are not generating anything to reuse. But at that stage, we were happy with the opportunity to make some cash each month while having a happy customer on the side.

Mradul, who was leading the assessments team, agreed to take this on. It was complicated and demanding work because each question had to be precise. It was not an easy business to deliver on. But we continued doing it for a couple of years till we got back on our feet. A chance meeting with an old friend and our team's flexibility to do what was right for the long term ensured that we kept getting money to help CoCubes get back on its feet.

From 2011 to 2013, I continued to put on weight. While I was not fat, I was the heaviest I had ever been, at about 85 kilograms. My pants had become tighter and I really didn't want to borrow money from my parents to buy new ones. In the auto, bus, metro and occasional taxi rides, I would loosen the belt a little to make sitting more comfortable. On a trip to Bangalore to meet an important client, the combined stress of an unhealthy body and an overthinking mind became so much that, on alighting from the cab, I vomited right in front of the client's office. Thankfully, I managed to do the deed in the bushes. I wiped my face, gargled in the bathroom and went to the meeting.

That day, I got it into my mind that if I made myself leaner and fitter, our company would also become leaner and fitter. This thought became the pivot around which both CoCubes and I started to get healthier.

thirteen

turning it around

I n April 2013, at the end of the month, the money in the bank was about Rs 5 lakh.

Our first goal was to find a way to get through the lean season. We had brought down our monthly cost to Rs 35 lakh from Rs 1 crore. But it still wasn't enough. A boon came in the form of a tax refund from the government. Our clients deducted some part of the tax upfront and deposited it with the government. Now, because we were a loss-making company, there were no taxes to pay and the government refunded this amount. In 2013, this was around Rs 50 lakh and came at the right time to tide us through.

In July 2013, we conducted our first major town hall after moving to the smaller office and outlined a three-step approach for taking CoCubes ahead. It included the following points:

- Reduce costs.
- Increase revenue to become profitable.
- Conduct experiments to find the growth path.

We shared with everyone that we had completed the first step. There were no more areas left for us to cut costs in. We were actually beginning to grow again. Most companies shut down once their venture capital is exhausted. We had fought and were now moving on to our next agenda.

This was to build a profitable company in 2013. The feeling that we could run a company without the external support of cash was liberating. Even the anticipation came as a relief. We had aligned the entire team's incentives in a way that it was dependant on the company being profitable. The third point was about hope—that we would not be satisfied with only becoming profitable, and that we would continue running experiments and growing our market size.

One such experiment was building an automated platform for evaluating coders. For the longest time, multiple choice questions followed by a detailed interview had been used to shortlist students. But it was now possible to build an engine which automatically evaluated a candidate's coding abilities. This was the main experiment we picked and pushed forward to get clients. It took one large, new customer acquisition to get everyone to believe that we would make it as a company.

This customer was Microsoft. They had a huge RFP process, and every assessment company had applied therein. For all our competitors, this was another potential customer. But for us, as founders, this was a matter of life and death. We knew that if we could get Microsoft to adopt our online assessments, that positive wave could sweep us back up. It could get team members to believe that things would work out and assure our other customers that we were still out there, winning. We worked hard, we ensured that we answered every question that the client had, we had a solution for every operational problem—and we got the deal. In my twelve years as a start-up person, I still think that was the hardest sale we made and the sale that I really gave everything to.

And it had the desired impact.

Slowly, money started flowing in. Because we were charging for our services now, a lot of customers left, but enough stayed. We were delivering value to them and asking for a reasonable price. The entire leadership team had stood by us during this time. Almost everyone had foregone bonuses and taken salary cuts to make this work. As our marketing and customer-support lead left, Ishita Mehta, who was the head of HR, took these functions up to ensure that we could keep our costs down.

From 2012–14, we struggled to meet payroll deadlines. The last week of each month would always be spent trying to get enough cash in the bank to meet salary expectations. But we were growing each month. By March 2014, we had reached break-even and were even probably a couple of thousand rupees in profit. We were profitable because we had no other choice. Being profitable is a different feeling. It has the power to make you feel free.

We got the team together and shared that we had crossed the deepest part of the valley of death but that we were not yet out of the ditch completely. As a seven-year-old company, we had already weathered two recessions, but with a new government coming to power in May 2014, the mood in the country was positive. Businesses were willing to experiment, and we needed to seize this opportunity.

One of the major changes that had come about in the company (and this was a lesson to remember) was the change in focus from asking 'What's new?' to 'How can we be better?'. Rather than working on more features and new products, we focused on how to make our single offering more valuable for the customer. This focus had an invigorating effect on our renewal rates, which had gone up from 30 per cent to 80 per cent for colleges and up to 95 per cent for corporates.

During all this time, as we were struggling, we had tried to sell our company with little success. We realized that no one wanted to pay for any of the assets we had imagined in our heads. While some conversations were still going on, we had learnt that companies can't be sold—they can only be bought.

Entrepreneurs are hopeful by nature. We spend so much time and energy in building our company that we believe we have created something valuable. I belonged to that category for a long time. And then when a third party doesn't value that, it hurts. That no one considers your life's work to be valuable can be deeply disappointing.

I think that is when, as an entrepreneur, you have a choice: to really listen to what the person in front of you is saying or to keep living in your delusion. When over the course of three months we kept hearing that what we had was not valuable, it really made us think. What the buyers were seeing was a bunch of youngsters who had been in the news for a short while and had built a company over five years. A company which had made a million dollars in revenue but had spent 2 million dollars in the last year. It was not only the cost of buying but the cost of running the company that mattered to them. They also saw a lot of customer names but low retention rates. One useful outcome of others evaluating us was that we understood the metrics that really mattered to them. And those were the metrics we were not doing great at. We thought we had a great team, which was true. But with the product market fit missing, there was literally no value for these softer aspects of business. A 'product market fit' is said to have occurred when you have a product which can satisfy the market and which reflects in happy customers. Our renewal rates had been low, which meant that we had unhappy customers, which in turn meant that we didn't have product market fit.

So over the next couple of years we went on to fixing those metrics, bringing our customer retention rate from less than 40 per cent to greater than 90 per cent. And this held us in good stead when the final buyer came along.

fourteen

a long conversation

In September 2013, we got a call from someone in Aon. She wanted to schedule a meeting with the head of Aon's assessment team in India. I didn't think too much about it and went ahead. It was a good short meeting with Vikas, who was leading the business at that time, and Sushil, Aon's marketing head. There were discussions around what CoCubes was doing, what were our offerings to customers, etc. At the end of our talk, we decided to find ways to partner and started exchanging emails and opportunities.

Aon had multiple entities in India. The biggest entity was the human resource outsourcing business with 10,000+ people. While they had been a customer since 2010, the relationship had deepened due to a chance encounter. In 2012, I was invited by Adil Nargolwala to a party at his house. Adil was leading recruitment at WNS and both of us shared a love for running. There were a lot of runners there that evening, and at this party I met Jasjit Kang, who was the CEO for the

HRO business. We spent the evening chatting about fitness and agreed to meet later. In our subsequent meetings in Jasjit's office, our relationship with the HRO business deepened. In Aon HRO we had a happy customer.

After my meeting with Vikas, we tried to find ways to work together. We explored our options and maintained a cordial relationship. Vibhore and I understood that Aon and CoCubes could be a good fit. But we knew from experience that raising the question of 'Do you want to buy?' was not the right approach. So we kept working on CoCubes. Growing revenue and making the company more profitable month on month. Then, in February 2014, I met Vikas for coffee at CyberHub in Gurgaon. We spent some time chatting about a few clients we could together pitch to. Then, as we warmed up, he asked casually if we would be willing to explore a deeper tie-up? I asked him what he meant by that. And he said, 'I don't know, but it could go in any direction.' I think we both understood what he was saying. I said, 'We would be happy to explore.'

February 2014 was when our conversation started.

2014: Getting the India Leadership Team On Board

Vikas introduced us to Nitin Sethi (a partner at Aon) to take the conversation ahead. Within a couple of weeks he had visited our office. He came across as a straightforward guy. We liked him instantly. After the meeting he said that he would go back and figure out the next steps. Two months passed by. Meanwhile, we had been nominated as one of the top ten innovative products in India by InTech and kept sharing such positive updates with Aon. This was one of the things that we did well during our entire conversation. We were quick to share internal updates and business reports, as well as testimonials from customers, with Aon to ensure there was a positive feeling at all times.

In July 2014, I wrote an email to Nitin asking for a status update so that we could inform our investors, as this aspect was still open. He replied, saying that there was progress and scheduled a meeting for us with the entire India leadership team of Aon. Vibhore and I went. We spent a pleasant hour with about eight folks in the Aon conference room, explaining our business. It seemed like the meeting had gone well and we came back happy. Our understanding after talking to the Aon team was that from here on out to getting a term sheet, the process would take about eight weeks. So we thought that by October 2014 the deal would be done.

At this point, we also filed our annual results. We were now profitable. Because the clients took time to pay, we were still struggling to get enough cash in the bank each month, and this was the biggest driver to continue the conversation in the direction of selling the company.

By August end we hadn't made much progress with Aon. So I pinged them again. Nitin replied, saying he had a meeting scheduled next week with the global stakeholders in Singapore. He got me in touch with Pritish in his team so that we could make a deck together, which Nitin could then present. He came back from Singapore and we met. The meeting had been positive. Aon was keen but a fairly conservative company. So the valuation multiple they were looking at was 2–3x of the revenue. This means that they were proposing to buy the company at two to three times our revenue number. I mentioned that this might not work for us and that we would have to speak with the board and come back. We discussed this internally. While none of us liked the number, it did mean that we would be able to pay back our debt and return all the money we had raised, plus make some money. So we went back to say that a minimum 3x of forward-looking multiple would work for us. A 'forward-looking multiple' meant that we were asking them to give us a valuation multiple of the sum of revenue for the next twelve months rather than the previous twelve months. By the time this discussion occurred, we were four weeks into the eight weeks stipulated. Also, the festival season was approaching, which generally leads to things slowing down.

It wasn't till late October that Nitin put us in touch with the finance team at Aon to start the initial diligence. The eight weeks that Vibhore and I had thought of as the initial target had come and gone. But we convinced ourselves by saying that big companies worked slowly. And at least we were making progress.

What was also making progress were our assessment solutions in the market. A lot more students and colleges had started taking our assessments. And on Quikr there were listings of tutors willing to coach students to clear the CoCubes exam.

2015 Q1: The Initial DD—Meeting the Finance and Technology Teams

By 10 November 2015, the finance team had shared its initial checklist with us, which included things like the shareholding pattern, the key monthly information reports, the organization chart, the financial accounts and tax details. We knew that Aon was a fairly conservative company in terms of growth, one that valued profitability. So to avoid any unnecessary attention, we shared a safe plan which allowed for about 28 per cent growth and a similar level of profitability as we had now.

We were also introduced to the technology team at Aon. It took us two months to get the DD questionnaire from them. This was a big detailed Excel questionnaire which had five sheets with about 100+ rows in total, with each row translating to significant work at our end. It took us five days and nights to fill this in. By the time we explained everything to the person leading technology and built a relationship, we learnt that he was leaving Aon. This had been a major reason our technology DD had been getting delayed in the first place. Now, we had to almost start all over again.

By then our decision to work on making the company profitable had started to show results. In the last week of March 2015, I wrote an email to Nitin sharing that we had agreed on a valuation multiple of 3x but that six months had passed. So the 3x now had to be used for the following year's revenue projection. Aon replied, saying that they understood there had been some delay and agreed to look at this. Because we were growing at a rate of more than 50 per cent, it meant that with every passing month, we became more and more expensive to buy.

At that time, a case study on CoCubes was published at Harvard. Debolina Dutta (one of our clients) had been working on it as part of her PhD, and it came through at a good time for us. We also hired a PR agency to increase our visibility in the news for a few months; we would then use these clips and share them with the stakeholders within Aon.

Given that the conversation with Aon had been going well, we reached out to other possible acquirers, sharing that there was interest in our company, and that if they moved fast there could still be a deal. We started engagement with three large global companies. But while there was initial interest and conversations, it was clear that no one was willing to bite so soon.

2015 Q2 and Q3: More Time, and a Shock

April, May and June flew by. A lot happened in these months.

The Aon India leadership formally met our board members in April. Aon had mentioned this as an important step before giving us a term sheet. This meeting had gone well. But by May we still didn't have a term sheet, so we wrote an email, formally asking for it. We got a reply saying that it would take two to three more weeks for Aon to get there. We had by now accepted that large companies with so many different functions moved slowly. This was not a start-up, and this was not the key responsibility of the folks who were on it. This was unexpected work that had come to them.

On the personal front, things had been busy. Bhakti and I were trying to have children. (Vibhore has always had it easy in such cases. He has made simpler choices. Like with regard to kids—*I don't want to have a kid*.)

We were expecting now and, for Bhakti's birthday in August, we decided to embark on a babymoon to Russia. As we were preparing to leave, Nitin called to say that Aon India was finally ready. But the term sheet couldn't be given by the India team; it had to come from the central mergers and acquisitions team in the US. While this was new information, it didn't matter to us. We just wanted the term sheet. He introduced us to the M&A team, who proposed a date and time for the call. Bang in the middle of the babymoon—4 a.m., St Petersburg time.

To say that the call was interesting is an understatement. I dialled in at four in the morning as the US team said that it would be good to be introduced to each other, and that they were looking forward to knowing more about us and evaluating the company. They also said that they would schedule another call to take this ahead. I replied in a calm voice that it was good to meet them too, but that I believed the purpose of the call was to get a term sheet from Aon— because everything else had been done, including a discussion on valuation. I think the US team were shocked; they replied saying that this was not possible. No one from Aon, except the M&A team, could do any DD or talk to another company to acquire them. Now, it was my turn to be shocked. But I could do little on the call. So both sides decided to touch base again and I hung up the phone.

I called Vibhore to tell him about this turn of events. I then wrote a message to Nitin sharing what had happened and how surprised we were by this development. After this, I caught up on some sleep and then woke up to go see a Russian palace.

After Bhakti and I came back from Russia, things moved fast. I think the US and the India team found common ground quite quickly. On 14 August 2015, the US team told us that they would come back with a formal offer.

August rolled by. September came around. There was no word. The Indian Aon team also didn't have an update.

It had been eighteen months since we had started engaging with Aon in this direction. And now that we were supposed to finally get the term sheet, the Aon M&A team had vanished.

There were some more positive developments on the side. There was now interest from a private equity firm to invest close to $5 million and take 30 per cent ownership in the firm. Internally, while I was keen to sell CoCubes, Vibhore was okay if we raised the capital and built a larger company. This feeling had been intensifying for a while. Both of us were beginning to get bullish with regard to our business again. Our revenue run rate had close to doubled in the last twelve months. This had energized us, but we were looking in different directions. I thought about this as a good way for a larger exit, but Vibhore thought of it as a chance to again build a 100+ crore revenue company. There was some dissonance, but given our friendship, we were talking it out regularly. Communicating frequently with each other is what got us so far as friends and partners. We shared this with the private equity firm and they were okay with me moving on and Vibhore taking charge. This was a good deal.

With all this happening in the background, Aon was still moving at a snail's pace. We called our board to convey the same to them, saying that this was now distracting us from our business which had started to do well. We were growing. We were profitable, with customer-retention rates of over 90 per cent. And we decided that we would say no.

I don't remember now whether it was a tactic on our part. But I do remember that we were really prepared to walk away.

On 16 September 2015, we sent an email to the Aon M&A team.

Hi,

We just wanted to let you know that we would not be interested in taking this conversation ahead.

Thanks.

Regards,
Harpreet

We forwarded the same to the India team at Aon.
Then Vibhore and I went out for a beer.

fifteen

project dollar

Nitin called us within an hour. We had just finished our afternoon beer. He said that while he was surprised to see the email, he understood where we were coming from. He added that we should hold on till the end of the day.

In another couple of hours Nitin called to say that a meeting had been set up for the evening. The head of M&A was keen to speak with us. We agreed to take the call. We lost nothing by doing that.

On the call, Aon shared that they had been involved in doing a big deal in the US and hadn't had the time to spend on us. But this was important for them. And they wanted us to move forward. We responded by saying that it had been a year and a half since we had begun discussions, that this slow movement was distracting for us. Also, in the first half of the year we had grown by 63 per cent, so the existing valuation didn't work. Aon said they were willing to look at all this if we could share our updated projections for the future. By midnight, we had sent them our future projected revenue, which was almost double of what we had submitted earlier.

In hindsight, the size of the deal was both a boon and a bane. Because the deal size was not hundreds of millions, it could be done and led from India. But at the same time, because the deal size was small, it didn't get the attention of the global folks in the large company we were talking to.

Aon US scheduled a call over the next two days, sharing that they were considering the new data and would need two to three weeks to get all the approvals to give us a term sheet. We said all right and waited.

Mid-October, at the Mumbai airport, waiting for our flight back to Gurgaon after a meeting with a private equity firm, we got our first official letter of intent for buying what we had built over ten years.

Negotiating the Letter of Intent

It was a simple three-page LoI, laying out the financial details. As expected, the offer was higher than the earlier offer discussed over the phone. It was a real cash offer which had three components:

- The upfront component, which would be given while closing the transaction.
- The earn-out component, which would be given over three years.
- The retention for founders, which would be given over three years.

During the entire process, the M&A team also visited us in our Gurgaon office. We were still holed up in a shabby building and a small office. We were looking to move out but for now we were there. We came across as a small company to someone from the US; like a company that could appreciate a bigger, better office space with coffee machines, and so on. Though we had no such aspirations after our experience in 2012, I do think this impacted perception and hence the valuation.

After issuing the LoI, Aon obviously wanted us to sign it quickly. It was mentioned that the offer would expire within a week. We wrote back to say that we were interested and would discuss it with the board. The first thing that we had to then decide was whether we wanted to sign the term sheet from the private equity firm, or take this 100 per cent sale option from Aon. Vibhore and I went out for a walk. I was clear about what I wanted. I wanted to take Aon's offer.

After a few days of discussions, Vibhore got on board and we decided to sell.

One of the main things missing from the offer were the revenue numbers at which we would make money from the earn-out. This was critical because we could end up signing the offer and later these revenue numbers could be too high for us to achieve. Then we wouldn't be able to make the earn-out.

The other thing that we were uncomfortable with was the retention aspect over three years. Now that we were in the mode to sell the company, we wanted to sell and go on to doing other things. Three years was too long a period to do it. So we wanted to negotiate it down to one year. But Aon wasn't willing to budge. Everyone, including the business guys in India, were aligned on the position that as part of acquiring a company, they wanted the founders to stay. Finally, everyone agreed to a retention period of two years—that at the end of twenty-four months, a certain amount of money would be paid out to the founders if they were still with Aon.

Because this was a short LoI, it didn't cover points like what would happen if Aon asked us to go after twenty-two months. They could come up with a reason to make that happen because they would own the company. This was important because there was a significant amount of money involved, more than Rs 10 crore. But we attributed trust to this acquisition that was being done by a global brand who wouldn't pull off such a thing.

Aon also asked for all the shareholders to sign the deal. A lot of angel investors owned small bits of equity. We didn't want every shareholder to know about the deal yet. So we spoke to Aon and agreed on only signatures from the founders and Ojas.

It was December 2015 by the time all of these issues were resolved and integrated into the LoI. Signing this document now meant that the course of the company would be set. But there were folks who had spent the last eight years building CoCubes with us. It was important to get them on board too. Most of the work done with regard to collating data, arranging meetings, and so on, had been under the pretext of raising more capital. Only Sameer and Nilay knew that a discussion of this kind was on.

Once we got the final, revised LoI, we called Sameer and Nilay to a dhaba for a chat over beer. They both owned a percentage each in CoCubes, and we wanted to get them on board. It was an emotional discussion, and their first reaction was to congratulate each other and say well done.

From being close to shutting the company down, we had come a long way. Five years ago, when Nilay had joined the company, his father had cautioned him not to work for a start-up. Two years ago, when the company had been in the dumps, Nilay had been offered permanent residency in New Zealand. But knowing how fragile CoCubes was then, he had let the moment go by. He had again been criticized by his family. Today, his decisions seemed to be paying off and he was happy.

Sameer is a fighter. He enjoys being in survival mode, where his best comes out. He was happy about the offer, but he said he hoped we wouldn't sell. The personal goal he had set for himself had been to get to Rs 1 crore in the bank by the age of thirty (which he had done). By forty, he wanted to get to Rs 10 crore in the bank, which was possible if CoCubes continued on its journey. If we sold, then, while he would make a lot of money, it wouldn't appreciate as fast as the equity would. We ended the evening drunk less on beer and more on emotions.

After this discussion on 18 December 2015, we sent back the signed LoI and thought about relaxing in the new year.

2016: Project Dollar

During the discussions on the LoI, we had continued to engage deeply with the Aon business team. By this time, Aon and CoCubes were also working together with a few clients, cross-selling each other's solutions. Both sides could see tangible monetary impact from the partnership. We planned a visit to the Philippines together to see how we could open up markets in which Aon was already present.

Opening up new geography takes time in a B2B environment. Our competitors had tried out the US, the Philippines, China and other Asian markets, but the revenues from these were still negligible in comparison to what they were making in India. Aon's global reach was a big draw for us to be able to take CoCubes outside India.

After we sent the signed LoI, the next step was the external DD. While the Aon India team had already done a detailed internal DD, now the diligence would be done by an external auditor. The first kick-off meeting happened in February 2016. This was code-named Project Dollar.

DDs are never fun. The questionnaire file had about 500 rows spread across various functions. We now had to assemble a small team within CoCubes to work on the documents. We roped in Nishant, who used to handle finance and data, and Karan, who managed product processes internally. We told both of them about the deal and got them working full-time on this.

While all this was going on, the health of CoCubes had improved considerably. We were no longer short on cash at the end of each month and we had taken a bigger office, paying Rs 4 lakh as the monthly rent. The space, in fact, ended up being in the same building as our earlier fancy office. The difference this time, though, was that we were doing 2.5 million dollars in revenue and were profitable.

At this point, I think a fortunate thing happened. Pritish, who was part of Nitin's team, was formally pulled in to work on Project Dollar. He was smart and worked harder and longer than us. And he took ownership of this project, which meant that he helped pushed the machinery within Aon to work on Project Dollar. Having someone as hungry on the other side was significant in actually getting the deal through.

I think it is highly fortunate if one is able to sell a business which is not making money. Because then there is nothing related to finance to really check on. Everyone is going by gut, and the diligence is minimal. Similarly, if you are being bought by a fast-growing start-up because of the conviction of the founder, the DD can be completed really quickly. Because the founder wants to really buy the company, everyone else follows suit. Selling to a big public company had all the hassles that come with it. For CoCubes, every client agreement was read by the auditors. Every financial statement for the last eight years was surveyed. Every conceivable metric was made and diagnosed.

Over the two years before the deal went through, there were a lot of times when we felt frustrated, but talking to Nitin would always help. Having been with Aon for fifteen-plus years he understood the system. He knew it was slow. I sometimes suspect he knew that this process could take so long, and that if he had told us this at the very beginning, we wouldn't have agreed to even start the discussion. Nevertheless, he was always available to chat. He was our champion internally and would always be okay to go out for a beer and hear us out.

We kept sharing internal and external positive news with Aon. By this time, we were sure that no deal is done till the time the money hits the bank. Till that point, we had to keep building confidence. We had also learnt a big lesson from the earlier term sheet that had gone wrong: *Work with the other team to make the overall deal successful.* If that means more work, then do it if you want the deal to go through. For several internal Aon presentations, we pitched in with inputs to all the folks who were working on the deal at Aon. We didn't shy away from helping create slides which accurately represented our business to the senior internal stakeholders. We were happy to review documents that were sent our way before they were shared with the larger team internally.

One of the most interesting features of our assessment platform was 'Eye in the Sky', which helped us monitor assessments in real time. More and more exams were happening remotely, and clients wanted to be able to monitor them in real time. It would have been easy to not have any name for the feature. But giving it one turned out to be a master stroke. Giving it an identity helped tremendously. Aon's internal pitch on our product revolved around Eye in the Sky. Everyone wanted to see its demo and it was mentioned in every meeting we had around the product.

Finally, in April 2016, we got the share purchase agreement. This was the final agreement that we would need to sign, which would mean that we would then be a part of Aon. This was cause for celebration.

The SPA validated the phrase 'the devil is in the details'. By the end of May, we had most of the issues solved, but I had pushed back so much that there was this perceptible negative energy between the teams. After twenty months of to and fro, I was also exhausted. At this point, we decided that Vibhore should take over discussions with the Aon team so that things could come back to normal. This helped and by the second week of June all the agreements were done.

But it still took till November to close the transaction.

There were so many last-minute things to keep in mind. The finalization of the share price, the depository slips, getting physical signatures from everyone, the mismatch of names on share certificates: the list was endless. Some of the early folks who owned ESOPs had forgotten about it. Some had moved to the US; many had changed their numbers. We tracked everyone down and told them about the transaction. We ensured they got the money they had, many years ago, believed they would make.

There were so many times when the deal almost didn't happen. I think the fact that we could afford not to sell the company was the reason we were able to sell it. We had the power to say no at all points in time. We were growing and profitable. Our plan B was to continue running the company. This gave us the confidence to push back on the clauses we didn't want to accept. We had a champion in Nitin at Aon who wanted to do the deal. Without Nitin, and the young team comprising Pritish and Dwiti that he put on the job, the deal might not have been possible.

It would have been great to have the input of someone who had sold his company to a public-listed American firm, but there aren't too many examples of those in India. Going back, if there is one thing we would want to correct, it would be to ensure that all the paperwork related to regulations is in tip-top condition. Over ten years, small things from each year had piled up, and each one had led to a delay.

During the deal we felt that the folks at Aon were slow, and at several points even felt that they may not be interested in proceeding. After selling the company and starting to work as a part of Aon, I realized this was the pace at which most large companies work.

Overall, it had taken us two and a half years to close this transaction. But finally we had sold our company. We had returned the debt we owed to people; our first angel investor made a 20x return, our VCs were able to get back 3x their original investment and our team members were able to participate in the upside with ESOPs. The shares which had been rendered worthless in 2012 had finally made some money. As founders, we had made a few million dollars each and could finally sit back and think about what to do next.

PART II

FOR THE
ENTREPRENEUR IN YOU

A. Personal Life

one

the married life of an
entrepreneur

t was the summer of 2011 and I was having the time of my
life. We had just raised a million dollars, I was on the cover
of *Inc.* magazine and Bhakti, my wife, had told me she
wanted to pursue an opportunity to work in Hong Kong
for a year. I thought: *What more could I want?* If Bhakti
moved to Hong Kong, it would free up more time for me to
spend on CoCubes.

We had spend the last four years slogging. Both Vibhore
and I had quit our jobs in 2007, raised some angel investment
in 2008, VC investment in 2009, and we believed in what we
were doing. I was spending my hours building a team, meeting
customers and investors, getting a new office and what not.
We needed forty-eight-hour days.

And if Bhakti moved to Hong Kong now, I could do more
meetings and come home later than before. Open the laptop,

watch a TV series over dinner and just get back to work and fall asleep while doing it.

Every month I would make a weekend trip to Hong Kong. Life would be awesome!

Three months passed.

I was alternating between *not* missing her and *really* missing her.

Everything started getting to me. It was good to have all the time in the world, and there were weeks when I wouldn't miss her at all. But then, not having someone to smile at you when you are finally home after a long day was a let-down. Takeout food was starting to irritate me; the butter chicken was just not tasting as good any more. I missed seeing Bhakti's face when I woke up in the morning. Just lying down for five minutes and looking at her. Hanging out with bachelors was turning out to be less fun each time, and most of my friends were married. I didn't like being a loner at parties, not having someone to hold, someone who'd press my arm to get attention and ask for a refill of dessert. I started missing that.

And I realized both these feelings were not good. Not missing your partner is probably worse than missing them. Because then, what are you partners for?

I called and asked Bhakti to come back. She said, 'You are mad.' I asked why. She said, 'Hey, look, you are so busy, you don't have time for me!' And I said, 'That's not the case,' fully knowing that that had been especially true for the last year that we had been married and the overall four since CoCubes started. She was absolutely unwilling to uproot her cool job in Hong Kong for the same thing all over again.

And I realized, it wasn't just a change of jobs for Bhakti. She had actually gone because, while I loved her, my actions had long stopped following my words. I had made her feel empty, with my mechanical actions. With anything and everything that I did, my start-up was always at the back of my mind, taking me away from the present moment. And this was when she had moved from London to India to be with me, then from Mumbai to Gurgaon, leaving her family and the familiarity of each subsequent place. She had been complaining about her job in Gurgaon, and I think I had just been mindlessly nodding all along. It had been a few years since I had written a poem for her, taken her for a surprise lunch, planned a long trip or taken a break to just be with her. We were speaking to each other but we had not *talked* in a long time. And she ran away. She realized that I was pursuing my dreams and so she chose to pursue hers.

I went and spent a week with Bhakti in HK. I hadn't seen her this happy since we had started dating in college. She was laughing abundantly, her face was radiant, she was discovering new things, the job was great, the money was 10x what she had been getting in India. I blended in. Activated my international roaming and bought Skype credit. While she went to office during the day, I finished my CoCubes stuff and picked her up after work. We went for strolls, hit pubs like teenagers, sat by the ocean and looked out of the window of our forty-eighth-floor apartment. I left notes for her around the house, picked up flowers on the way and enjoyed our evenings together.

We talked. Bhakti was not willing to come back to India immediately. She had a one-year commitment to the company. She said she would complete that time period and then return. And I don't think she was sure of how it would be once she came back to India. Would I really change and give her more time?

So I came back to India.

Bhakti's birthday was on 3 August, and I wished her over FaceTime. Seeing her celebrating there and cutting a cake with her friends didn't feel right at all. Nothing was worth this. I was sure that if this went on for a few more months, Hong Kong would take her away. I really loved her. It made my heart ache.

A week or so later, I packed up my bags impromptu. I called up my parents and took the next flight out and landed up at Bhakti's door. I said I was willing to do whatever it took but that I would not go back to India without her. And that we would go back together in a week. It was a horrible week. From fighting to crying to leaving a deposit of $5000 on the rented house to informing her company that she would be going back to India to answering frantic calls from both sets of parents. But somehow one week later we were on a flight back home.

The next few months were tough. Bhakti was angry, and rightly so. I was making tea in the morning and coming back home for lunch. I was coaxing her to look for a job, asking her to paint. It took time.

This was so many years ago. Building a company necessitated that we stay in Gurgaon where our entire team was. In 2016, after selling CoCubes, I was in a position to ask her what she wanted to do next. Which city did she want to live in? And she picked Mumbai. So a few months after selling CoCubes, we moved to Mumbai so that she could pursue her dream career.

I am happy that I did what I did and didn't budge till she agreed to come back with me. A year down the line, she told me that is what had convinced her to come back.

I had backed it up by really taking out time for her, by ensuring all Sundays were, and still are, always for her. If by chance there was something to be done on a Sunday, she knew about it well in advance, and I would make up for it during the week. We go on a big vacation every year.

Once I come home, I spend two hours not looking at my phone and laptop. And I am definitely more productive than before. This does not affect the running of a company.

I have been doing some angel investing and have friends who are more ambitious than me. I see them running companies and pursuing careers. I see in them what I was doing in 2011 every day.

Entrepreneurship gives a lot to the entrepreneur. But it also takes a lot from you. If you are an entrepreneur, pause and check what you are giving away. Stop looking at your phone when you are with your partner, don't take that call when you are out on a dinner date, take an annual vacation together, stop multitasking while chatting with your mom, dad, brother, sister and the love of your life.

Sometimes your partner will be upfront and tell you this on day two. Sometimes it might take a couple of years. And sometimes your partner will not tell you this even in twenty years. You will then look back and say that they 'stood by your side' while you stole time away. That is not enough.

So, at the very least, drop your phone for an hour and take out that Sunday. I can guarantee, your work will not suffer. And maybe your wife won't run away.[1]

two

co-founder dynamics: partner in crime

My wife calls Vibhore my girlfriend. It's a joke because that is the amount of time Vibhore takes away from me that I could have spent with her. The same holds true in Vibhore's household with regard to me.

As of 2020, Vibhore and I have known each other for twenty years. We were room-mates in college. The idea of CoCubes came to me, but it was Vibhore who had the balls to leave his job first. We built CoCubes for twelve years. We have survived a lot together, including becoming relatives (Vibhore married my cousin).

But it hasn't always been a smooth ride. The toughest time was in 2013, when we were going through hell trying to rebuild CoCubes. On top of it, our personal relationship was also strained. There were many small reasons, not worth going into because, in hindsight, they were not the real reasons. I spoke to my dad about how Vibhore and I were finding it tough to communicate and see eye to eye. My father said, 'Son, it is not about all this. It is about money.'

My dad had hit the nail on the head. Stress tends to spill over, and this was what was causing friction between us. Both of us had graduated from college eight years ago. Most of our batchmates were doing well and going on foreign vacations. And there we were, taking money from our parents to run our houses, because CoCubes was failing. I remember going to the ATM to withdraw 2000 bucks and getting a shock when the receipt read: *insufficient balance*.

'Once you get money again, all of this will go away,' my dad said. And it did.

In general, we have complementary skills. He is the guy who codes. I am the one who sells the code. That's how we started. I am always out there scouting for ideas. Then I come back and ramble on in a few directions. Vibhore helps us make the call. He brings in the clarity to be able to find that thread in a jumble. As the company grew, our functions became clear. I took ownership of operations, sales and HR, while Vibhore took ownership of product, technology and finance. We would always give feedback to each other but let the other person take the final call. This worked well in most cases, but it did get heated several times.

The part where Vibhore would question me would generally be about:

- *Increasing expenses*: I would take a bullish view, and Vibhore would calm me down. He would challenge me on the exact numbers we were looking to hire, if we really needed so many people, why were the reimbursements increasing, etc. The argument was that we were incurring too many expenses. After the first couple of fights, where I thought he was 'questioning' me, I understood that these discussions were helpful. He left the final call to me and, most of the time, we found the middle path.

- *How fast can the company grow next year*: These were challenging discussions. In the early years, we set unrealistic targets for a B2B company and always under-delivered. Then we became ultraconservative because we were short of cash and didn't want to get into a situation where we would run out of it, so each number would be thoroughly checked, each client renewal accounted for, each salesperson's list combed through. In the second situation, the question we got stuck over was this: Can we grow faster? Why can't the sales guys do more? What are we missing? As much as I hated feeling that I had to defend myself, I realized over time that it was a boon to have someone who could ask me tough questions and whom I was answerable to.

On the other hand, I would end up raising my blood pressure over the following:

- *Not being able to see the product that was being developed*: For the longest time, I felt that our product team should create mock-ups of what they were trying to develop and share that with the business team. This step would ensure that what was being developed was actually what the customer wanted. But Vibhore was opposed to that. He would patiently explain that such process was followed in large companies and that if we started doing the same, we would get delayed. I would generally reply by saying that we should hire more people. Over time, we found common ground by sharing sketches that the salespersons could use to keep the prospects engaged.

- *Not being able to hire techies*: This is something we weren't able to do well for a long time. My opinion was that since Vibhore was the co-founder, he should be able to build his own team. He, however, would rely on the recruitment team to help fill positions. But they reported to me, and a shouting match would then ensue, where we would blame each other for not being able to hire techies. Looking back, I think we should have had a specialist recruiter for techies who could have been in the recruitment team and reported to Vibhore for these positions. That would have solved the matter somewhat. Also, since I was the one out in the market and meeting people, I should have spent more time and energy in finding senior technology people there.

Apart from this, there were a lot of other areas that we continued to disagree on.

Who Owns Strategy?

I wish we were more in sync when we were deciding the strategy for CoCubes. Looking back, I feel that it landed somewhere between what I wanted to do and what Vibhore wanted to do. I believe it is better if the buck stops with one person within the company. Vibhore doesn't feel the same way about it and continues to believes in co-ownership.

Who Gets Media Visibility?

In 2012, just as we raised our second round and our concept of connecting colleges and companies was gaining popularity, *Inc.* magazine wanted to feature some of the promising companies of India, and CoCubes was nominated. They called us for a photo shoot, where we met Amar Goel, the founder of Komli, who was getting featured too. The photographer took pictures of Vibhore and me together, then took pictures of the three of us and then a couple more of me with Amar. It was a nice experience and we came back happy. When the magazine came out, I found myself on the cover with Amar, while Vibhore and I were featured together on the inside pages. This was one of the few times that we got into a serious fight. It was over visibility.

Vibhore was of the opinion that we shouldn't have agreed to separate pictures. I was of the view that we should do whatever is required for CoCubes to get visibility, and at no point should that get compromised. I believed CoCubes should get as much free publicity as it could, it didn't matter how or who got it. So if we were applying for an award where only one founder would be invited to get the award, I would say let us go ahead. But Vibhore's view was that we should participate only where both of us could be featured, or push the organization or publication to feature us both. I thought this was a waste of energy, and this led to disagreements for a few years.

I think it was easy for me to say this because I was not the co-founder who sat behind a desk (or in our case, in a coffee shop) and got stuff done. I was the 'face', the founder hogging the limelight and getting media attention. This can, and does, create conflict in a lot of cases. The situation becomes more complicated when it involves your family and relatives. If the 'face' is on TV and the other founder's family watches it, they wonder why s/he weren't there instead.

I don't think this is a theoretical issue but a real one that needs to be addressed between co-founders. I believe that while everyone enjoys getting featured, not everyone enjoys the process. If someone is writing a story on start-ups in your sector and talking to multiple start-ups, they are likely to write positively or give more exposure to the one where they had the most positive interaction. The ability to be liked by the journalist doing the story is a skill, and the founder who can build such a rapport should take on this interaction. Having the same person featured again creates continuity and subsequent retention in the minds of readers and other entrepreneurs, so having one person take centre stage is in the best interest of the start-up.

Vibhore, however, believes otherwise. His view is that one should avoid such conflicts, and in the long run, an extra article in the newspaper or an extra award won't matter.

Where we both agree is on the point that co-founders should discuss this beforehand, so that they are on the same page when the media issue comes up. Have mutually-decided guidelines in place to follow and share with the marketing team. We didn't do it when we started and solely relied on strong friendship to tide over this difference in opinion, but that is best avoided.

Apart from these areas, where we were not in agreement, there were three things we did to ensure that we could work together effectively:

- *Same gain or loss*: One way we were able to ensure that there was no unnecessary financial angle to our discussions was by ensuring that we had the same stock, salary and bonus for the entire time we ran CoCubes.
- *We never disagreed in public*: There were times when we didn't agree with each other. Innumerable times. But we never cut each other off in public. We used these times to talk to each other and understand each other better. And fine-tune our relationship for the future.
- *We kept each other's word*: If one of us committed something to a team member, investor or customer, it meant that CoCubes had committed. Whether that was a salary-hike decision or a feature that had to be built. This just meant that it was all the more important that we were on the same page most of the time.

Over time, we have seen that we have become mirrors *of* and not *for* each other. We often find ourselves starting at opposite ends of an argument and realizing that we have convinced each other to switch positions. It's quite a funny situation!

The chemistry of the co-founders makes or breaks a start-up. The clearest indication that something is not going well is when you can't say what is on your mind to your co-founder. If you ever find yourself in a position where you are unable to talk to your co-founder, you are in trouble. In that case, simply go and talk to them. There is no other way. When you can say it out loud, then, suddenly, the tension disappears from your mind. It is out in the open and you can work on it together.

Finally, understand what you are working towards. It is easy to be on the same page when things are going well.

It is when things go awry that differences start to arise. In 2013, when our mutual stress spilled over, what saved us was that both of us really wanted our friendship to be okay. With the emotional turmoil of the family and team members taking a toll on us, the last thing we wanted was our friendship to be affected. And it had started getting to that point. This is when both of us backed off and started talking again. We found paths for the growth of the company that were more agreeable to both of us. It is possible that this compromised the growth of the company, but we did ensure that we got our friendship back on track first.

three

having a coach

I n 2007, when I started the company, I was twenty-four years old. I felt that I could take on the world alone. I hated being in a position where I'd need advice. Someone suggested that I should get a mentor, and I scoffed. I saw no need. Lines from Robert Frost's poem 'The Road Not Taken' rang in my head: 'Two roads diverged in a yellow wood . . . I took the one less travelled by, and that has made all the difference.' I didn't feel like I needed advice, what I wanted to do was just *do*.

I did think that maybe the company needed a mentor. Someone who had built a company before, sold it; hired people, fired people; seen the highs and lows and emerged alive from it all. In 2007, one of the few places you could approach for help was TiE. We were introduced to Vivek Agarwal, who had earlier built and sold eGurukool to NIIT in 2003. After a few interactions with Vivek, we offered him 0.5 per cent equity in the firm to be a mentor. But it was clear that he was a mentor for the company, not for me.

In 2009, we raised our first round from Ojas Ventures; Raghu and Gautam from Ojas joined our board. Among the other things that we are grateful for, they introduced us to T.V.G. Krishnamurty. TVG helps founders. He was presented to me as someone who could help me make decisions. Sounded like a coach to me, except I didn't want one. I met him and found him to be polite, but I didn't follow up on our conversation at all. He gave me some next steps to do and they slipped my mind as I went back to building a company. Gautam followed up. I met TVG again; I met him because I liked him in the first meeting, and this time around the conversation was better. He was seventy years old but full of infectious energy.

I started calling him occasionally, to share the problems I was facing as a founder. During one of the calls I told him about my weaknesses and how I planned on working on them. TVG stopped me right there. He told me to focus on my strengths and amplify them; meanwhile, he suggested I find team members whose strengths could complement my weaknesses. This was really helpful advice.

I asked him how I could work more efficiently with people with a high IQ. I felt people with high IQ behaved differently in the organization, how they had a tendency to show more ego within teams, how they could be bad communicators and needed a lot of self-time and space. He helped me with that as well.

But it was in 2012 that the importance of having a coach really hit me. Because that advice saved our company.

Our venture capital deal had fallen through. To help the company survive, we had taken on debt which was not supposed to be risked. We had to let go of 60 per cent of the team members, but we helped them land other jobs. At that time, we thought the only way out was to sell the company. So we sent emails, got leads, made visits and took expensive last-minute flights at the remotest chance of a meeting. We pushed the pedal in that direction for a couple of months.

We had a million dollars in revenue then, we had access to more than 300 universities, 200-plus corporate customers and over a million students. But when someone knows you are in a desperate situation, the only thing you will get are lowball offers. Folks got us over to chat and just learn about the field, with no real interest in pursuing the conversation; big job boards (like Naukri.com and Monster.com) told us there was no market size.

Vibhore and I had not taken salaries (we did accrue them though), the leadership team had taken heavy salary cuts. One of the things we were extremely embarrassed about was moving the office from a fancy location to a no-name building. We moved from a 7000-sq. ft office with a training room, boardrooms and central air conditioning to an 800-sq. ft office with one air conditioner, a meeting-room-cum-pantry that could only seat three people and desks with no room to rest your elbows on. We had to reduce the size of our desks to fit another row to seat people. From going to the pub for drinks, we were now walking across the road to a dhaba to eat dal tadka and roti. Our competitors had started to reach out to our customers to tell them we wouldn't survive and so they should switch. We were getting calls from our top customers and had to fly out to meet them, buying plane tickets with money we didn't have. I remember being overwhelmed by all this: explaining to team members, to customers, to my family, to friends. I remember thinking: *I am glad I have a co-founder*.

On one of those days, I was sitting in the fire-escape staircase of the office building. An office that we would leave the following month to shift to one that was one-tenth its size. I was talking to a client who, over the course of business, had become a friend. I was telling him about our situation and he said, 'Sometimes it doesn't work out. And it is okay to quit. You have a long life ahead of you. You can do a lot of things.' It was well-meaning advice. I remember thinking, *Maybe he is right. Maybe it is okay to let go*. But our hearts weren't prepared to do that.

And then I remember the call that helped me focus. The call that helped me get rid of all the other thoughts of trying to sell the company, of trying to get people and customers to stay, of talking to the landlord to give back our deposit, of trying to think about what to do next, of trying to meet the payroll deadline. It was a call with my coach, TVG. He had listened to me patiently as I rambled on about this and then he said, 'Harpreet, you and Vibhore are smart guys. You have a good team. I am sure in the last five years of building the company, you have built something valuable. So just focus on protecting that asset. For the next few months just protect and grow it.'

That changed everything for us. It got us thinking: *What is valuable in our company?* We got into a room and thrashed it out. It turned out that nobody else had a larger distribution system in colleges; very few companies had relationships with recruitment managers in companies like we did, and we had a database of over a million students. We realized that by bringing them together, we were adding value, but because we had been funded by VCs and were moving towards a larger purpose, we were not charging for that value. We had been credited with destroying the corporate assessment market by offering it for free to corporates for the last two years. So we decided to start charging for our online assessments. One thing led to another and we turned around our company to become an online assessment company.

In 2014, as CoCubes got back on its feet, I grew restless—this was not the company I had really wanted to build. My dream was to help more students choose their career path, do a lot more engagement with them online. But, as an assessment company, we had dived deep into B2B sales and the market size seemed limited. So one night I wrote to TVG, asking him what I should do next. I explained how I was invested in CoCubes's original idea and that I felt that I should spend my life pursuing it; though the path would be harder, it would be worth it.

In the morning, he replied: 'You can never make a decision for your entire life in just one instance in time. There is always a trade-off. The key is to be aware of what you have traded off. And no regrets. Let the body speak; hear your emotions. If you're continuously out of sync, change course.' This was brilliant advice which helped take the burden off my shoulders of trying to make a decision for a lifetime.

It has taken me a lot of years to realize that as one builds the company, it is not the company which needs the most support—it is the individual(s) building the company. As you hire people, spend time in raising money, take time away from your family on weekends, and are left with no time to spend with your parents and kids, the person most affected by all this is *you*. You are the one processing information constantly and reacting to it.

And a lot of times, what is best for the company is not the best for you. If the company is at a stage where it demands high growth, and you have been building the firm for ten years and feel tired, what is the best choice? To hire a CEO? To refocus on the company? To sell it?

Many times, what is best for the company is difficult to do. If the company is not able to raise funding, or a new division you launched isn't working out, maybe it is best to let go of people immediately. But the emotional cost of doing it can weigh you down. Decisions like these, when delayed, can kill a company.

So, as you go through the emotional journey of being an entrepreneur, having someone by your side—who has seen these situations before, who has no vested interest in the company but only in you as an individual—can be invaluable. They can help you think through difficult choices, they can help you and/or your co-founder think clearly.

It has been three years since we sold the company to Aon. The other day, I wrote to TVG again. I said: *I am struggling to choose a path between a company that will grow very fast and build a large global presence versus building a company over time by being the master of what to do, how to do it, with a small, good team which is happy doing it. How do I choose?*

He replied: *Why do anything? What's the motivation? That is the place to start. Then decide on the* how. *What route to take to get there. Which one makes it faster, more certain, etc. All these will depend on* why. And this answer, as always, brought me clarity. It helped me step away from my own chaos and told me to answer the why.

As we worked together, I asked him about taking equity in CoCubes, but he refused. So I asked him, 'Why do you do what you do?' For many years, he said, 'Because I like solving problems.' I pushed harder, I kept asking why again. He finally relented and told me a story about how he lost his glasses while boarding a plane to Australia last year. Just before the plane took off, he called an entrepreneur whom he had worked with to turn around a spectacles factory in South East Asia. TVG asked him if something could be done. By the time he landed in Australia and reached his hotel, a new pair of spectacles was there. The person had figured out the prescription number, and got the spectacles made and delivered to prevent inconvenience to his coach. TVG said, 'I do it because I like such relationships.' I have never received a call like that from TVG. But I hope I do.

So I ask you, if the founders of Google can have a coach, why can't you? And if you do, I wish you find somebody like mine.

four

just because we can

I came across a line in a book which immediately struck me: *We do many things in life just because we can.* And I thought this was so true in daily life and even more so in the life of an entrepreneur.

I took a flight to meet a prospect in Chennai. I thought if this was thirty years ago, going to Chennai would have been such a long trip. But now, because I can hop on a plane in the morning, conduct a meeting and be back home by night, I don't think twice before saying yes to a meeting in a faraway city. Just because I can go. I am sure this spurs the GDP and all the numbers that we keep tracking, but is this the best use of my time as an entrepreneur?

Just because we can check with our team members on the status of a deliverable at any time of the day doesn't mean we should. Just because it is easier now for someone to drop a hi, get in a cab and come by doesn't mean we should meet.

Doing all these small things gives one the illusion of being productive without really making a material change to the fate of the company. It makes you feel like you have done so much, ticked off so many tasks in a day. But the things that get done this way are the easiest ones, things that should ideally be solved by giving more autonomy to your team, hiring better people and managing your time better. In doing the easiest things, what gets left out are the hard decisions—the search for a new sales head, the decision to let go of a poor performer, the decision to work on a new product, the decision to think through the business model, and more.

An entrepreneur's life is busy. Sometimes it seems like a hard slog, day in and day out. One meeting after the other, seven missed calls when you step out of a meeting, so many mails to reply to, so many stakeholders to manage. I realized that being connected all the time actually meant doing what the world wanted me to do. I had to struggle to really find time for the three things that I wrote down as important for the company in the morning. At the end of the day, the amount of time we have is limited. An entrepreneur should spend it on the things that will make an actual, significant difference to the company. And not take a meeting or a random call just because we can.

B. The Biggest Asset: People

one

---

building culture

This is a chapter that we really wanted to write well. Because after ten years of running the company, if there is one thing that we are proud of, it is that we built a company which had good culture. But what was this good culture? Why did we feel so? Why is having good culture important for any company?

How and Why We Were so Fervent about Building a Great Culture

Around the time we started CoCubes, we came across an article in the *New York Times*. It was an interview with Tony Hsieh, the CEO of Zappos, titled 'On a Scale of 1 to 10, How Weird Are You?' In it, he was asked about the most important leadership lesson he had learnt so far. He answered that the real reason he and his partners had sold their company, LinkExchange, to Microsoft for 265 million dollars was because the culture at the company had gone completely downhill.[1] When they had started, it was like a typical dot-com. They would work, 24/7, without any idea of what day of the week it was. But by the time they got to a hundred people, even though they had hired people with the right skill sets and expectations, he dreaded getting out of bed and going to office. Because he didn't feel great about it.

As young entrepreneurs, this was eye-opening for us. Vibhore and I discussed this over our daily chats and agreed that we wouldn't let the same happen to CoCubes. That we would build a company where people wanted to come in to work every day. A company that its team members could believe in and found worth spending time on.

The Need for Good Culture

Let me quote from Ben Horowitz's blog entry.[2] He's one of the founders of Opsware, and of the venture firm Andreessen Horowitz.

> Let me break it down for you. In good organizations, people can focus on their work and have confidence that if they get their work done, good things will happen for both the company and them personally. It is a true pleasure to work in an organization such as this. Every person can wake up knowing that the work they do will be efficient, effective and make a difference both for the organization and themselves. These things make their jobs both motivating and fulfilling.
>
> In a poor organization, on the other hand, people spend much of their time fighting organizational boundaries,

infighting and broken processes. They are not even clear on what their jobs are, so there is no way to know if they are getting the job done or not. In the miracle case that they work ridiculous hours and get the job done, they have no idea what it means for the company or their careers. To make it all much worse and rub salt in the wound, when they finally work up the courage to tell [the] management how fucked up their situation is, [the] management denies there is a problem, then defends the status quo, [and] then ignores the problem.

Culture has a high impact on everything. And every company has a culture. The only decision founders need to take is to decide to create it knowingly.

What Culture Is Not

One of my juniors from college started a new venture in 2014. Their team started out of college, keeping costs low. But within eight months, they were able to raise Rs 15 crore in funding. The team moved to an office which could accommodate 200 people. There were beanbags, a table tennis corner, coffee machines, standing workstations and cool decor. More than half the office was empty though. A venture capitalist who invested in the company said that the reception of the new office was bigger than the venture capitalist's office. The company, which was burning Rs 1.2 crore a month, shut down in 2016, unable to meet revenue numbers and raise more money. When the start-up-funding boom happened in India in 2014 or so, suddenly, young founders were raising money on paper plans. And the first thing on the agenda after raising money was building an office. This was said to be cool and, somehow, many founders felt that this was an important aspect of the culture.

Here's the thing, though: culture is not a fully centralized AC office designed with vibrant colours. It is not a fancy coffee machine or a laid-out lunch buffet. Culture is not a ping-pong or air hockey table. Culture is not material comfort.

You might feel that these things will help you with hiring. But the truth is that you can't throw money to build a cool office and say that we have great culture. You don't suddenly get venture capital and develop great culture. Actually, that is when you almost always lose it. Because hiring dilutes culture.

What Is Good Culture?

Culture can be easy to feel but difficult to describe. Let's say, you go out to a restaurant to eat. You enter the place and you feel welcome. You feel like you will be taken care of during the time you spend there. But if you were asked why you felt that way, there would be no single answer. Was it the way the person opened the door? Was it the correct lighting? Or was it because of the way the seating was done? Or the right music? It is none of those things alone and yet it is all of those things.

To get it right there are a million small things to take care of. And as founders you can't take care of all those small things. So what can you take care of? You can create a place of trust. A place where the people who work there believe that the company will keep their interests in mind before taking any call. A place where they will be listened to. A place which is more than just an entity to create economic wealth.

Trust

'I trust you' in a company means that I am willing to take a risk on your behaviour. We can create this trust by devising a set of common values. Having common values, which everyone agrees upon, encourages consistent behaviour. It allows us to believe in the reliability of others. With this comes the possibility of cooperation. This consistent behaviour becomes your culture.

Consistent behaviour

Belief in common values

Company Culture

Trust

Culture gives everyone in the company a common language. The greater the number of team members who trust that common values will be upheld, the more consistent will be their behaviour and that of the culture in the organization. On the other hand, a company where mutual trust is lacking will consistently see inconsistent behaviour. Inconsistent behaviour will make it harder for the company to achieve its goals.

How Is Trust Built?

Trust works both ways. Trust is what team members should have in their CEO, that s/he will put their interests before any personal interests. At the same time, there needs to exist the reciprocal trust that the company is hiring people who believe in putting its interests first. This seemingly paradoxical position is what creates trust. It feeds off the other, leading to a place where people can work with maximum emotional security. This is important in creating an organization with great culture. And this is why hiring and retaining the right folks is critical to building vibrant culture.

This kind of trust is built through both small and big instances. When I asked the team what culture meant to them, Kunal Bedarkar (who worked in our corporate sales team) shared the following incident with me. Some of us were in a meeting with the sales heads from different regions when Kunal's phone rang. It was his mother. We were in the middle of a presentation, and he cut the phone. I saw that and asked him why; he said it was because we were in the middle of a meeting. I asked him to step out and return the call. We believe that family comes before work. If your family is calling you at work, please take the call. For the rest, keep them aside. But here was a case where the team member thought of doing what was right for the company first, and the company thought of doing what was right for the team member. Such instances build deep trust and respect.

The time this theory was really put to test at CoCubes was in early 2013. It had been a few months since we had let go of 70 per cent of our team. We had already shifted to a smaller office and were trying to meet payroll each month. When we had raised venture capital funds, one of the senior folks who had joined us was Alok Rustagi. He had joined to lead the management of corporate accounts and online assessments. At that time, our key value addition to colleges was jobs, and in the last semester, the pressure to get companies to hire from our partner colleges was high. Every college salesperson would keep calling Alok to ask how many companies were willing to hire. Could they go to Odisha to hire? Could they travel to Bhopal?

Alok came and spoke to me. He had a great job offer from a niche consulting firm to join them as vice president, and he wanted to take it. I asked him to give me a day to think it over. CoCubes was in a shaky place, and the company was being held together by trust. That trust had been broken once, when we had asked so many people to leave, so the remaining team members now looked up to the leadership team (not the founders) to see if they would stay. Alok was extremely respected, and losing him would mean a lot of other folks also losing faith and leaving. We had just begun to see a turnaround. If Alok left now, there was a high chance that everything could crumble.

I met Alok at Downtown, a brewery in Gurgaon. I told him how I felt, that I understood why he wanted to move on. But I did add that if he moved on now, all the effort we had put in together over the last six months to save the company would go to waste. I asked him to stay on for another six months, at the end of which I offered to personally call anyone and everyone I knew to get him wherever he wanted to go next. He agreed to stay on. I believe this was a defining moment in ensuring the revival of CoCubes, and it was only possible because of the deep trust we had in each other, that we would look after each other's interests in the worst of times.

I read this somewhere and it has always resonated with me: 'Trust is the emotional glue that holds every team together. In times of trial, it transforms a group of committed individuals into a team of individuals committed to each other."[3]

Good Culture Is Not a Guarantee for Success

There are many companies which operate like mercenaries, where getting to the end economic goal takes precedence over everything else. These companies succeed too. Having good culture does not automatically ensure success. But it is a damn good way to:

1. Have fun while building the company.
2. Increase your chances of success if all the other things (market, timing, product, etc.) are right.
3. Get insurance if things don't go according to plan.

When we were trying to raise our Series B round, I floated the pitch deck to our existing investors and some other senior people for review. Most of them felt that the last slide was unnecessary; many felt that it should be removed so that we didn't come across as a soft company. The slide was about our company culture. I had set out what our values were and how proud we were of our team who really believed in the vision that we had. In my head, it was meant to convey that we had a high chance of success because we had a passionate and committed team. We thought of it as our most important asset for succeeding.

Except that none of the audience thought the same way. They felt that it wouldn't matter to any of the future investors. I was quite surprised. But I realized that they weren't wrong. It wouldn't matter to the financial investors. Most of them didn't care if the people working in the company bonded well or not, had fun or not, reached their potential or not. They cared about making a return on the money they were investing. And that's fair. But I realize now that putting in that slide on culture in your presentation is a great way to spot an investor who would fit in, one who believes as fervently as we do that the culture at a company is important.

creating the culture at cocubes

It Is Important for People to Know That What They Do Really Matters

CoCubes was in the business of jobs. While most of the things were handled by technology on the back end, there was manual work too. We did campus hiring at scale and there would be on-ground invigilators handling candidates. After assessments, the companies would use their logins to declare the results.

In 2014, during one such campus drive in a premier college, the company HR person used the help of our account manager. He asked him to help download the Excel file with the assessment scores of candidates and apply certain filters to shortlist the right ones. Our account manager promptly shared the Excel file. The HR person took a printout and posted it on the noticeboard. In the next thirty minutes, we got to know that a final-year student had committed suicide after finding out that he had not been shortlisted for the next round in his dream company. And about the same time, our account manager realized that he had made a mistake in putting the right filters in the Excel file. He freaked out, and understandably so. We calmed him down and had a look at the revised Excel sheet. A few more names had been added but that student still hadn't cleared the assessment. But it was nerve-racking.

This is a true story that we shared with every new hire in our culture session to help them understand that the role they would play was critical. It is not just about logging in and pressing a few buttons on Excel. The impact of their actions is far higher, and hence what is expected from them at all points is of great importance too.

CoCubes Seven Values

Once, we decided to list down our values and ended up with a list of seven. We were serious about implementing these. Every joinee had to attend a culture session of one hour with the founders, where we walked them through what each value meant and why it had been included in the list. Everyone would then get their personal culture certificate and sign it and hang it up on their desks. Having a common set of values that everyone in the company knew was of paramount importance in getting the team to work together without friction towards a common goal.

It helped us build a company where there was transparency and the team members could openly talk about what was on their minds and in their hearts. This was also our first value.

Value 1: Speak Up

We encouraged a little dissent. We were of the firm belief that most problems in both our personal and professional lives stemmed from not being able to talk freely. If a team member was able to talk without fear, they would also be able to put in their best work. If someone didn't enjoy the role they were assigned, the person could let us know and CoCubes would find another role that might better suit him/her, or even help them find another job. We wouldn't just cut the person out. We told everyone that we didn't expect to stay our entire life at CoCubes, and neither were they expected to do the same. The only expectation was that till the time they were in the company, they should give it their best.

We also wanted all the team members to know that CoCubes trusted them from the very beginning. A new person joining CoCubes brought with them a fresh pair of eyes which could help us improve old processes and tackle problems with more creativity. Hence, it was important to implement this value so that everyone would know that all opinions were respected.

Value 2: Do What You Say

If there was one thing which was valued above everything else at CoCubes, it was this: *Doing what you said you would.* We believe this is a great indicator of the long-term success of any executive. In 2012, as our company expanded, we came to rely on Excel files. We created elaborate processes mapping each and every step. We captured metrics across entire process flows in files and used them. This led to a slowdown in execution. As we built the company back from scratch, we let go of these files. We relied on the value of 'Do what you say' rather than pore over an Excel file. It worked. It also led to deep friendships being formed based on the trust derived from this common value. We learnt that having too many processes before finding the product market fit slows down growth, and that relying only on trust pursuant to finding the product market fit will also do the same.

Value 3: Always Know Where You Are Heading

Alice's Adventures in Wonderland by Lewis Carroll is the story of a little girl who falls down a rabbit hole into a world populated by peculiar creatures. She is lost and comes across a fork in the road. On the side of the road is a cat. Alice asks the cat, 'Where do these roads go?' And the cat responds, 'Where do you want to go?' To which Alice replies, 'I don't know.' The cat then says, 'Then it doesn't matter.'

One can spend all day on a laptop without knowing exactly what the end output is. As a company grows, random tasks and the random assignment of tasks grow as well. By including 'Always know where you are heading' as a value, we wanted to pass on two messages. One was to the leads: that they should ensure that their teams were always in alignment with where CoCubes was heading. The second message was for every team member: that they should only do the tasks if they understood how the end output would be useful to the company. If they didn't get a satisfactory answer from their leads, they should raise their voice and ensure they find out.

Value 4: Know How Money Is Made

We believed that the more each team member understood how the money was being made, the more it would benefit

CoCubes. We had an assessment creation team which worked on creating new questions for assessment. And we would tell them that if they wanted to know how much their salary could grow in their current role, they needed to understand the rupee value of each question created. To understand that, they needed to understand how the questions are bunched together to make assessments. Furthermore, one should be able to understand the average price a client is willing to pay for a single assessment. What are the average number of questions in a test? And how many times can a question be used before it is archived? Because if you are able to create 200 questions in a month and the rupee value of each question is X, then there is no way your salary can be more than 200x. It is important for you to know what that limit is and what the opportunities are within or outside CoCubes when you are nearing that limit. We encouraged each person to check the value of their role in the company. This helped us tremendously during appraisals, and team members had a high degree of self-reflection as well.

Value 5: Innovate and Experiment

Remember the person we meet in family gatherings? The middle-aged person, who maybe has a kid and works in an IT company, and talks and walks slowly.

Now make a vow that you will never become that person. That you will stay hungry. That you will not work in a job where you are not learning. But also remember that the onus of learning lies on you.

One of the examples we used to illustrate the trap of 'not learning' was to talk about the pre-sales role at CoCubes. In this role, a team member had to call up companies and convince them to hire from our pool of assessed candidates.

So when someone joined in this role, they would get a list of the companies to call and then start cold-calling. Without fail, in most cases, the person would get bored after two, if not four, months and ask for a change. They would say that there was nothing more to learn here. Most of the time, when we looked at the data, over the last four months, their conversion rate wouldn't have improved. When they joined, they would have had a 3 per cent conversion, and at the end of four months, it would be without significant improvement. This showed that the person had neither innovated nor experimented in the role. It is easy to get bored in any role, unless you start to experiment.

Value 6: Have Fun

In his path-breaking book *Free to Learn*, Peter Gray writes that the best work is play, and that play is always conducted in an alert, active but non-stressed frame of mind. It is easy to build an office where everyone has to dress formally, talk slowly and just look at the computer screen in their cubicles for eight straight hours. But such an office can't really be the place where the best work of someone's life can be done. By including fun in the culture, we wanted to enjoy what we were doing. If folks enjoyed what they were doing, if they actively made friends in the office, they were more likely to stay on.

Value 7: Remember that 'Customer Is God' (Listen, Understand but Not Necessarily Obey)

Companies run on the money that customers choose to pay. So it is important to hear the customer. It is important to respect the customer. But we need not always obey the customer. This is because the customer, a lot of the times, can be wrong. One example of this was the feedback we got from our customers on the assessment platform. CoCubes had taken the unconventional route of showing all the questions of the test on a single page. This was different from our competitors who allowed a single question on each page and then the option of pressing 'next'. Our account management team would keep telling us that the customer was asking for one question per page.

We called a few of our customers, asking them why. Their answer was 'to prevent cheating'; they said that if two candidates were sitting next to each other and they had only one question on each page, they wouldn't be able to cheat from one another. What our customers did not know was that on our platform, the questions were randomly chosen from a large data bank, so the chance of having the same question paper for two candidates sitting next to each other was minuscule. Additionally, the question number, as well as the answer options, were randomized. Upon hearing this, 90 per cent of the clients were okay to use the platform the way it was designed.

The lesson here is that customers tend to generally offer solutions rather than share problems with the provider. So by including this in the culture statement, we wanted to tell everyone that while we respected our customers, it was important to not listen to them blindly. This value reduced friction between the operations and product teams as it provided common ground for them to deal with the customers.

The Biggest Threat to Culture

The elite coaches will tell you this: exercise makes you weak, recovery makes you stronger. Practice runs or a strength workout doesn't make us stronger, the after-effect of it does. Similarly, hiring makes culture weak. It leads to the 'strangers at a cocktail party' problem. This is described well in the book *ReWork: Change the Way You Work Forever* by the founders of Basecamp:

> If you go to a cocktail party where everyone is a stranger, the conversation is dull and stiff. You can make small talk about the weather, sports, TV shows, etc. You shy away from serious conversations and controversial topics. A small, intimate dinner party among old friends is a different story, though. There are genuinely interesting conversations and heated debates. At the end of the night, you feel like you actually got something out of it.[1]

When a company hires a lot of people together, we end up in a place where people avoid conflict. People avoid challenging each other's ideas. People do not open up their heads and hearts. This is also the case with large companies. People in large companies are too polite. Open disagreements are rare. In such an environment, it is impossible to work together to deliver a product that customers will love.

In a start-up, hiring slow is a great way to ensure your culture stays steady. If you have to hire fast, do realize that your culture is getting diluted and that you can make several interventions to ensure it stays intact.

Culture in Hiring, Reviews, Culture Bonus

Once, after our annual outing, I sent this email to the team:

> *Guys, we have withdrawn the offer that we made to Raghav [name changed to protect privacy] for Mumbai corp sales.*

The reason for that is the lack of meeting the benchmark for professional attitude that we have set at CoCubes.com, which directly impacts his gelling with the team. More than a couple of persons mentioned an incident where they were not comfortable interacting with him. We still think he is a good sales guy, just not for CoCubes.com.

Raghav had joined only three days before this email was sent out. On his first day, we had gone to Rishikesh for our annual team outing. I don't remember what exactly happened there, but by the end of the trip several people had walked up to us and the HR person, saying that this person was not right for our firm. We collated their comments and took a call. We called Raghav the following day, gave him a month's salary and asked him to leave. During his interviews, he had come across as a great salesperson, but now it seemed like he was not the right cultural fit. Such incidents showed that we were serious about the company's culture.

Every person joining the company spent time in the other functions, not just their own. This was so that the person who joined could genuinely understand the business. The best folks in the firm conducted the induction training for the new hires.

We didn't hold back people who wanted to leave. We never gave them a counter-offer. Someone wanting to leave is the final outcome. The decision to do so would have been made long back, and if someone had made the effort to go ahead and find a job, we wished them luck and helped them on their way.

There were no individual awards. No employee of the month. We believed that the final outcome was the result of a lot of team members and functions working together. And rewarding one isn't about making that person feel good. What it does is devalue everyone else who also worked hard. Also, it promotes a culture where people showcase work to become employee of the month or get a mention. That is dangerous in a start-up.

During our annual reviews, a person who had performed well individually but hadn't done well culturally was not promoted. It was clear to that person that it would be impossible for them to get to a place where they would manage people at CoCubes. This was difficult to do as a start-up. Several times, there were salespeople who brought in a lot of money but lacked discipline. They didn't do what they said they would. During the initial years, we found it hard to penalize a great salesperson. After all, he was bringing in much-needed money. Our competitors, too, had been after him to join them. But over time, we realized that this sent out the wrong message to everyone in the team, and we ensured that if a person was not culturally aligned, they couldn't become a team leader.

Creating Pride in Our Mission: Silver Coin

At the end of probation, every team member was given a real silver coin. This coin had the CoCubes logo on one side and the following line emblazoned on the other side: *I impact careers*. The coins cost us about Rs 600 each. We got them made because we wanted everyone to believe in the long-term vision of the company. And people felt proud to have it. It was a symbol that we were all in the same boat, sailing towards the same goal. We kept it in our wallets and showed it during our client meetings. This was not meant to win deals, but it did help us bag a lot of them. It created immediate trust. From the way the team member took it out of the pocket and showcased it, it was obvious to the customer that this person believed in the product being sold.

Making Families Part of the Celebration

Start-ups take up so much time that families often get ignored or left behind. The last thing we wanted to do was run a company where the employees didn't have the support of their partners or parents. We made families part of our celebrations. Our joys and sorrows. We wrote letters to the parents of the folks working with CoCubes, thanking them for being a part of our journey. If someone's parents were in town, we would encourage them to bring them to office and spend some time there. We made a WhatsApp group of all the husbands and wives of our team members and invited them to our parties. They were invited to join us on our annual trip as well. Many a time, a team member would go home after a long day's work only to find that their partner already knew about the celebration happening in the office the following week. We endeavoured to create as little division between friends, family, fun and work as possible.

Doing What Is Right in Company Policies

It is difficult to create camaraderie in a company which has a thick policy rule-book. Where policies vary by levels and positions, it results in everyone not being treated equally. We tried to keep our policies to a minimum. We trusted people. Integrity was valued. We told folks that it would be impossible to check each and every bill that they submitted as expenses. But if we did and found even 1 rupee that could not be accounted for correctly, they would be asked to leave. In our ten-year history, this happened twice, and we let go of the person immediately because of integrity issues.

Our policies were the same for everyone. There were no categories for senior and junior folks. Founders and leads stayed in the same hotel that a new hire would stay in. Rooms were shared. Everyone had the same meal allowance.

We had a lot of outstation folks. But we never got an office outside the head office in Gurgaon. Instead, we chose to give outstation employees a monthly per diem which they generally used to get a deal with a coffee-shop owner. This was a win-win. This ensured that the team members were mostly visiting client offices, or if they had to park themselves somewhere, the company was paying for those expenses. And if they didn't spend all of it, they could take home the rest of the per diem.

Being Fun

It is always easy to go on a trip. Book a resort, take a flight and leave. But it is difficult to create an experience that someone will remember, and we put in a lot of effort to make that work. In 2013, our annual trip was to trek and spend a night in a tent at Triund in Himachal. Everyone had been working super hard for the last couple of years and had put on weight. The climb took six hours, but the view from the top was beautiful. A lot of people cursed the choice of location. But this released into our culture an idea of being fit. When we talk about our off-sites, this one comes to mind immediately as it led to many people at CoCubes adopting a healthier lifestyle.

We were serious about having fun: if it was a Diwali bash, you had to be dressed appropriately. If you weren't, you either went out and bought a set of traditional clothes or went home to change.

At the entrance of our office was a board which read: *We don't have a receptionist. Please walk in and talk to the first person you see.*

Sometimes we got some gifts from colleges or corporates. So we used them to run an auction within the team. The items varied from a business-class ticket to Europe that we won from Lufthansa to office chairs. It was super fun. The collected money ended up being used for office parties.

For their birthday, each team member was told to take the day off. This is such a simple thing, and I wonder why other companies haven't implemented the same.

Culture Being Tested

In all probability, the start-up you build will go through a down phase. During an up phase, the team members have all the reasons to stick with your company. But when the chips are down, all those reasons vanish. And the only reason one will stay with you is because they like the job that they do.

In January 2012, Nilay Kothari was leading the technology team for Vibhore. His brother was based out of New Zealand and he had just been approved for permanent residency. Two months later, we had to let go of 60 per cent of CoCubes. Nilay's wife, parents and brother were after him to quit and move to New Zealand. But in his mind, it didn't feel right, because he was happy at CoCubes. He liked the people and he believed that the leadership team, even in times like these, knew what they were doing and get the company out of the dump. He went against what his family was telling him and took a salary cut to continue with CoCubes.

For a team committed to achieving something great together, sacrifice is essential. The key then is to create a culture and mission worthy of such a sacrifice.

three

leadership hiring

At CoCubes, as of 2018, the leadership team had been around for an average of six years in our eleven-year-long journey. It is possible that because the company grew slowly (60 per cent year over year) over the last five years, as opposed to growing fast, a lot of folks in leadership had the time to grow with it. At the same time, the folks in the leadership team stood by the company through thick and thin, took salary cuts and worked hard, day and night, to make the company a success.

Having a good leadership team makes a difference in two ways:

- By bringing in someone who can probably do the job better than you, you are helping the company grow.
- But more importantly, having a good leadership team is synonymous with having a personal life. A good leadership team enables you to take time off to spend with family, on

hobbies, etc., without worrying about how the business is doing. This can help you go further in your start-up journey and prevent a burnout.

We had a lot of misses in our leadership hiring, but we got better at it with time. Pursuant to raising venture funds, we decided we needed senior people to do sales in corporate. We hired a woman who had been running her own business in recruitment consulting for fifteen years. We realized that:

- After slowly growing her business for fifteen years, it was difficult for her to adjust to our pace of work.
- Being senior didn't necessary translate to leadership.
- Our product required 'concept selling', which hadn't been a requirement in her older business.

While she seemed like a great senior hire, it actually turned out to be the opposite.

Can We Go Out for Beer?

In start-ups, you will end up spending a *lot* of time with your leadership team. So much so that they will take up more time than you spend with your family and best friends and, if all goes well, you and your leadership team will become best friends. You can't be in the same room discussing the next quarter's strategy or going in detail over each prospect while thinking, *I don't really like this guy.* This is not about skills for the job, this is about getting along and complementing each other. So apart from everything else, a good question to ask yourself when making the final hiring call is this: If I had time, would I want to spend an evening with this person?

Does the Team Like the Person?

While trying to hire a senior person for college sales, my first email sharing information about CoCubes had Amit copied on it. Amit was our star college sales guy and I wanted him to be comfortable with the person we were hiring. I wanted him to be involved in the process. Whenever we have hired leadership folks at CoCubes, we have gone back to the team and asked them what kind of person they would like as a leader. What skill sets should s/he have to be able to lead you? Who would you respect and like? As part of the interview process, we ensured that the candidate in question met at least two to three people from the team that they would manage. In most cases, we had the senior person shadow a call or a visit with a customer so that both got a chance to do a 'real day' together. All this ended up giving us an insight into the person being hired as well as informing us about the team's thought process.

EQ Is As Important As IQ: Sharing Actual Feedback

1. Dedicated, hardworking, has his/her heart in the right place.
2. No doubt on your ability as a salesperson, good individual sales guy.
3. Lack of specific industry knowledge.
4. S/he has not managed a large sales team: Will s/he be able to hire a large sales team and manage it?
5. How will a young guy be perceived by the college as a leader?

The text above is from the email I sent to Sameer Nagpal after his final interview for the position of sales head. We used this email to discuss how we felt about the decision. It helped to ensure that everyone knew where they stood. He understood what part of his skill was valued, what expectations the firm had from him, what challenges he would face and what skills he would need to build were he to join the company.

Being a leader is as much about EQ as it is about IQ. To succeed, a person needs to be self-aware about his strengths and weaknesses, and also be able to take and give feedback. Sharing the actual feedback of interviewers with the person told us a lot about how they responded to criticism and praise, and helped us make a decision.

Does Their Family Support Their Decision?

When we were looking to hire our first operations head, I tried getting Ravi to join in. I had met Ravi during a client visit and pitched to him that leading operations at CoCubes would be a good role. He was keen but not sure if his family would be okay, so I volunteered to come down to his house and meet his parents. I did so and it was a pleasant hour that we spent together. While he did not join us immediately, in six months' time, Ravi wrote back to say that he was keen and joined CoCubes full time.

A start-up takes your life from you. It occupies your mind, it occupies your soul. If you have made the right leadership hire, then the person would be spending days and nights thinking about how to make the company succeed. The weekdays would be busy and soon the start-up would begin eating into weekends too. And this will be time stolen away from family. And this is only when the times are good.

If things go bad, the same person will be working harder, along with taking a salary cut. All of this, we believe, is not possible to do without a family which supported the original decision of the person joining the start-up. We always made it a point to meet the family of the person we were going to hire in a leadership position.

Do Our Values Match?

A person's values determine his/her management style. If your company believes that you should delay vendor payments as much as possible, till the vendors come home begging, you need to hire a person who is comfortable doing that. If, in your company, you believe that a new hire has as much freedom to speak as an older team member does, but you end up hiring a senior member who believes in authority, there will be a mismatch and people will leave. Hence, it is important to share the core values of the company with the candidate and ask them what their core values are. The kind of questions you can ask depends on the role, but a couple of general questions that we found helpful were:

- How would you deal with a person in your team who submitted a fake bill of Rs 100?
- You have someone in your team who had been performing well earlier but over the past month has been slacking. What conversation will you have with that person?

Do the Personal Aspirations Match the Company's Vision?

Over the course of years of hiring, we realized that while having the right skills for the job is important, it is also critical to ensure that there is a match between what the role offers and the personal aspirations of the candidate. We did this by:

- Sharing in detail how we saw the role evolving over time; what kind of revenue would the person have to build and manage, how many people in the team there would be.
- Sharing details on where the company was headed; whether we were looking to raise capital, how much cash did we have, were we profitable, why the idea might not work.
- Asking the person their expectation of annual growth in terms of compensation. How much should their salary be three years from now? What part would be fixed and variable going forward? If we went through a tough time, would they be okay to take a salary cut? This also helped us understand the financial position of the person. It is important because some folks have home loans or have to finance their kid's education—it might not be a great idea for them to join a start-up in that case. Then we could share upfront what we felt and how hard it could potentially get, so that the person can make a more informed choice.

Getting a good leader is invaluable. But getting someone who is not a fit can cause destruction, including causing the next layer of employees to leave. Keep your eyes and ears open to sense if that is happening. Spend a lot of time integrating the executive into the team. That is as important as hiring. And if it isn't working, don't let it drag. Let it go.

four

common mistakes made while hiring

Making Hiring Decisions on the Basis of Personal Bias

When trying to hire Sameer Nagpal, I found out that he did not meet his parents when he was in town for our interviews. I found that to be quite odd. I come from a family where this could be considered sacrilege. More importantly, I thought, could he become close enough to CoCubes? Would he bring the passion required of a leader and the love for the organization? Thank God I didn't act on that bias. One reason I think I didn't was because he came through a personal reference.

People whose first instincts are right are rare. If that is you, then, great. Maybe as an experienced person, having seen the world, your gut generally serves you right. But that is not the case for most people working in a company. So as the company grows, building a process to hire people, which avoids biases in interviews and looks at facts, will help. A process which doesn't judge a person by the way they dress or if they have tattoos or piercings. You could do this by making a list of the skills your company wants for the role and create questions around those skills. Then ask these questions and see if the person being interviewed has the skills for the job and a personality in tune with your culture. Make an objective choice. What you want to avoid is people in your company hiring on the basis of a gut feeling.

Hiring an HR Person for Your Start-up

We learnt about the importance of having a person who can communicate our passion to people, both within and outside the company, when Ishita Mehta joined us in 2011. She had joined in the dual role of HR and recruiter. With her around, our leadership team could start focusing on taking the company forward while she ensured that high-quality candidates didn't drop out. She took our help where it was required, she shouted at us if we postponed recruiting calls for client meetings, and she ensured that everything related to HR got done.

Start-ups don't need an HR person. Start-ups need a great recruiter. Someone who can:

- Create a pipeline of candidates from various channels.
- Excite every individual in the pipeline by conveying to them the passion you have as a founder.
- Ensure that the company respects the time of the person who is applying for an interview.
- Finally, close the loop and keep the person enthusiastic till he joins the company.

This person can then also function as the HR department, which covers, among other things, background verification, formulating policies, ensuring the salary structures are computed correctly and disbursed on time, and so on.

The HR role is generally considered a soft role. A role that is given to someone who will do all the process-oriented work required to be done. And most folks looking to become HR are loath to do the work of a recruiter. It is considered to be below their dignity. What start-ups need is a kick-ass recruiter who can also function as HR, and not an HR who will hire a recruiter to work on the open requirements.

Hiring Only A+ People

One of the most consistent bits of advice on blogs for hiring is to 'hire only A+ people' or 'only hire people who are better than you' or 'hire people so that the overall IQ in the team goes up'. This is not bad advice. But this confused us a lot while hiring as it is incomplete advice. We now believe that it is important to raise the bar when hiring new team members, but it is not necessary to have an 'overall better' person. What is required is to hire a person who is A+ in the skill that is most important for the role for which the person is being considered. Not overall.

Hiring for Seniority

As a company grows, it needs people with experience. As entrepreneurs, we imagine in our heads how the role might grow. How will the person we are hiring today manage more people tomorrow and build complex processes that will stand the test? In all cases, it is important to step back and really think if you need that senior person now. Can't the founder continue doing it for some more time? And more importantly, is there a young person in the team who is culturally aligned and who you can help progress to this role?

If you can make do with an internal person, there is nothing better. By doing that you send a signal to the entire team that if one works hard and smart, there is a way to progress faster. When you hire someone from the outside, you send the opposite message. The internal person will likely cost less and be more culturally aligned. Both are good reasons to give the job to the internal person.

Whenever we made the choice to hire a senior person from outside, the thing we found most useful was to discuss the matter with the team concerned. And to take feedback from clients who the hired person would interact with and would have to sign up or manage. The more buy-in we had from the people to be managed and the clients, the better were the chances of the senior person to succeed.

Hiring a Person Who Has Done It Before

I found this in a LinkedIn post by Brian Fink, an American technical recruiter, and I think this summarizes the matter well.

> When you hire somebody too early who has already 'done it', you often find somebody that is less motivated in tough times, less willing to be scrappy . . . more 'needy' and less mentally flexible or insufficiently willing to change their way of thinking.[1]

On the other hand, hiring someone and giving them a chance to punch above their weight gets you a person who is as motivated as you are to succeed. Someone scrappy who would be willing to change to succeed with the company.

Because hiring is about people.

There are many mistakes one can make. A subpar team member is a big cost to the company. You can't build a company if you have a leaky bucket of underperformers or high attrition. Hence, spending time on hiring the right people who stay is critical for a company's long-term success.

five

hiring slow. firing fast

Hiring fast and firing slow—this is what founders do most of the time. When we feel our company is growing, we hire quickly. And when we have too many people and the revenue is not growing, we still believe in luck.

But what we should be doing is just the opposite. We learnt this the hard way.

Hiring Slow

In a start-up, as the annual strategy gets decided, generally, the projections for the coming year's revenue show high growth. Excel files for the budget and the headcount are prepared. Given that the revenue is increasing by a lot, it naturally indicates that the start-up will need a higher delivery bandwidth. And so the hiring starts. But then salespeople don't get hired in time, but the delivery folks do. Now, you have a bloated delivery team, while the sales numbers haven't improved much.

In addition, if you have raised venture capital, it is easy for a lead in the company to say, 'We are doing so many things. Work has increased, I need one more person to manage.' As a founder, you are busy, you want things to move fast, and the person asking is a trusted lieutenant, so you whip out your phone on the spot, and write an email to HR, approving the new position. You walk away feeling like you really got work done.

Damage Alert

We made both these mistakes at CoCubes, not once but several times. Moving fast for a start-up is essential and good. But when it comes to hiring, moving slow is better. Taking out the time to review each position, why it is required and the hiring process is time well spent. This is because:

- Adding each new person to the team dilutes culture. It doesn't make the company stronger but weaker.
- Great recruiters are hard to find. It is best to use their time in looking for the right hires. The ones that you really need.
- A bloated team is a slow team. Every hire slows down your team further.

Over time, we started applying a few parameters to see if we really needed another person or not.

Started Using Metrics

Our operations team used to service the clients after they came on board. This was the team which, in 2012, had swollen in size, and as sales failed to keep pace with the folks hired, we had to let go of people. As we matured, we realized that an operations person could manage client revenue worth Rs 1 crore. So we kept a metric of Rs 1 crore per operations person. So if we were doing Rs 6 crore in revenue, then we would need, at most, six delivery folks; and we started to hire only after we had reached that revenue number, not in advance.

Kept Improving the Metric's Efficiency

The initial metric was Rs 1 crore per delivery person. During the year, we asked our operations head, Ankur, to list down the things that could help him improve the metric to Rs 1.25 crore per delivery person. This is what he came up with:

- *Visibility on the sales pipeline*: This allowed the delivery team time to accommodate new clients by creating space and re-juggling work.
- *Change in the team structure*: We had a large-enough client base in the metro cities, and so the team head suggested that we change the team structure from headquarter-based to city-based. This improved efficiency and also provided a growth path for the operations team.
- *Tech requirement to improve efficiency*: This included simple macros and tools for daily tasks which could lead to the saving of man hours.

We would then implement these points over the year, trying to improve the metric further. This ensured that we were lean.

Tied Efficiency to Bonus and the Growth of Leads

Once a metric was established, Ankur's bonus as the head of operations was dependent on how optimized this system was. He was now effectively running a P&L. He signed clients who gave us a certain revenue and incurred delivery costs which he had to manage. The greater the profit, the better his bonus. A large part of the bonus component came from the percentage of profit generated. We also created a pool of bonus money from the savings made. A part of this money was split between the members of the operations team. So now when a team member was working hard, working on the weekends, they knew that this also resulted in a better financial impact for them personally, while helping the company overall. The team knew that if they were one person less, it meant a larger bonus at the end of the year. This was a win-win solution.

Having different incentive structures for each function is a luxury that start-ups have. This is a critical one-up that should be utilized to the hilt. Large companies simplify their incentive structures so that they are easy to manage and execute. But then they lose out because a person's incentives are no longer tied to performance.

Firing Fast

Many entrepreneurs will tell you that one of the hardest things to do is to ask someone to leave. We personally always felt a sense of responsibility for the person, their family, for their future. But we could always do it without guilt. Because our guiding light was clear to us—as founders, it was our responsibility to ensure that the company did well.

People are generally let go of for two main reasons.

Reason 1: The person is unable to do the job (either due to attitude or aptitude).

Reason 2: The company is not doing well.

Why Leaders Delay Firing

- *They find it hard on their conscience*: Many leaders personally feel responsible for the failure of the person in question. They believe they hired the person, they convinced them to leave another job, so now how could they ask them to leave? While this is true, the other side of the issue is that you made a mistake, and the sooner you correct it the better it is for the company.
- *They think things will improve*: Well, they don't. A person who is performing poorly because of a lack of skill doesn't gain enough domain experience or cognitive ability overnight, or even in a month. Things don't improve with a poor performer, they get worse.
- *They fear what others will think*: When I was working at Inductis and someone new was hired, as peers, we would know within a week if the person would fit in or not. Peers always know how a hire is performing, but the leaders get to know later. So don't worry about what the team will feel, they already know. On his blog, *Both Sides of the Table*,

Mark Suster has this to say: 'I have never regretted firing anybody. Not once. I have on many occasions regretted not firing somebody quickly enough.' He adds, 'Trust me: if you know, you know. If you know, do it now. Almost universally your staff will come out of the woodworks and say, "Thank you, he needed to go."'[1]

What to Ensure before Letting Go

Before making the final call on letting someone go, it is important to hear their side of the story. We had a team member at CoCubes who had the right skill set but was underperforming. An informal discussion revealed to us that she was in an abusive relationship with her boyfriend. That was the real cause for her dipping performance. Our HR and friends in the company helped her during that time and she got out of that relationship. Overnight, her performance improved.

Before letting someone go, a leader must ensure that there is genuine underperformance; don't go by just a gut feeling.

In a start-up, an important part of letting people go is communication with the team. We struggled with this for the longest time. The concern the remaining team members had was that the news of firing that person came as a surprise to them. And they heard about it from someone else.

So we decided to inform the team members as soon as someone exited the company. We wouldn't make up fancy reasons for letting the person go. We would say it the way it was. In our joining document, we included the following text as well:

Why is someone asked to leave? When do we take a call to ask a person to move on?

o   The person does not want to work hard enough (indicator is client delivery getting impacted).

o   The person is delivering below expectations (meeting less than 50 per cent of the expected output after training).

o   Discipline issues (the person works well, works hard enough in gaps but is not reliable for consistent delivery).

o   The person is a cultural misfit (multiple people have reported that they are not comfortable working with the person).

o   The person has integrity issues (data security, theft, lying, etc.).

It took years for team members to trust that at CoCubes we didn't let go of people without serious consideration; and that we always let go if the team member was not performing well enough—no exceptions.

It is important to treat the person who is exiting with respect. The person who is leaving has real friends in the office. It is important that everyone knows that, no matter what, the company will treat them like a human being at all points in time.

six

when people want to leave

The text below is from an email we sent out when one of our team members, Ankit, was leaving:

Guys and Gals,

Ankit [has] communicated that he wants to move on to a job in Accenture. His last day in the organization is the coming Friday. Before that, he will be spending time in helping us automate the process. He has been a great team member, always smiling and dedicated to delivering the task.

Over the last two reviews, Ankit had expressed a desire to code, something we have been unable to fulfil as a firm. Our best wishes to him for a great career ahead.

Party on Friday night, I guess, is obvious!!

There is a saying, 'People leave their managers, not their companies.' I think this is true to a large extent, but not entirely. People leave for a lot of reasons. They want to pursue higher education, they want to move abroad or move to a government job; they get married, or their partner gets a job in another city and they move. The key thing we have realized over the years is that it is okay for people to leave.

As young start-up founders, for a long time, we viewed people looking to leave as some kind of betrayal, if not a personal failure. When someone wanted to leave, if the person reported to me directly, or was someone I knew well in the organization and doing well, I would come up with reasons for them to stay. I would do my research and tell them why CoCubes was the best option for their career. Sometimes it worked, sometimes it didn't. When it worked, rarely was the person as engaged as earlier, or stayed for long enough after the conversation.

Once a person has made up their mind to leave, it is difficult to change it back. They have made the effort to go out and find a job. They have spoken to their families and friends, explaining to them their reasons for changing their job. Now, even if what you are saying makes sense to them, to really accept it will mean acknowledging to themselves and to their friends and families that their original decision was incorrect. This kind of acceptance is hard. Therefore, it is possible that because of your authority and the need to maintain a good relationship in the future, the person might say yes, but they rarely stay long enough for it to be helpful to them, to you or to the company.

So the real question is this: What can we do so that our best performers want to stay?

Wishing Them All the Best

Once someone wants to go, and if they are treated well when they are leaving, they can safely return later, without their ego being pricked and any bridges being burnt. Within CoCubes, we had multiple such cases. Shipra Rawat joined in 2010 in the corporate delivery team. Parag Ghatpande joined in the college operations team in 2011. Both were good performers and stayed with the company till 2013, when they decided to leave. Both joined start-ups in a domain similar to CoCubes's. I take their names together because they met each other at our company and ended up getting married. A year down the line, both of them chose to come back, in 2014, with Parag joining the corporate sales team and Shipra returning to her original role. Both had matured more and brought in new perspectives which helped CoCubes. As of 2019, both of them were still with CoCubes. By treating them well when they were leaving, we had kept the door open for them to come back.

So when a person comes up to you to say they want to leave, wish them all the best and see how you can help them in whatever path they have chosen for themselves. Because the bus has already left, and the time to do what you could have done is gone. You can now dust yourself off and do things to ensure that the rest of the folks want to stay.

seven

common people-management mistakes we made, and some things we got right

Just as I sat down to write this chapter, the founders of a company I had angel-invested in called me. They had a situation on their hands. A star performer who was heading content and managing ten full-time people, along with fifty freelancers, did not get along with one of the founders (say, Founder A). Their working styles didn't match. The question the founders had for me was: Given the fact that she was able to do the role well and had taken on so much, should they consider getting her to report to the other founder?

I thought this was a bad idea. Assuming the working style of Founder A was coherent with the culture of the firm, this would signal to the rest of the company that if you didn't get along with one, you could just go to the other co-founder.

It's not unlike my experience with my four-year-old daughter sometimes. She will go ask her mother for something, and if she doesn't get it, she will come to me to check the same thing. It is important that my wife and I are on the same page, else my daughter just might end up eating chocolates all the time. Similarly, I believe it is important for co-founders to be on the same page.

Another reason I thought this would be a bad idea was because this meant that the founder who originally didn't want to manage content would now have to do so, which definitely is not his interest area. So the only option then is for the founder currently managing content to see if he can work with the team member and deliver results which are useful for the company. Or bite the bullet and let her go. Fight the battle now to avoid a war in the future.

These kinds of incidents ultimately have a large impact on a company's performance. And such decisions are numerous and often made in between client meetings and investors. We made a lot of mistakes in this area but also got a lot of things right.

Some Common Mistakes We Made

Rewarding One-time Performance with a High Fixed Salary Increment

A good reward system shouldn't reward a one-time great performance with a high fixed salary increment. It should reward it with a great bonus to keep fixed salaries in control and in line with the market. Having a great variable component helps keep costs in line with revenues, so that the company pays more only on continuous good performance.

Mismanaging Your Best People

Mismanagement mostly happens with your star folks, those you believe to be the upcoming leaders in your company. There are two sure-shot ways of mismanaging your best people:

- Giving them more than what they can handle and leaving them on their own.
- Putting them in roles where their skill sets don't match.

In a fast-growing company, when a new thread opens up, you call the star performer who is already handling several threads and give them one more thread. They don't say 'no' out of respect and optimism. But the jar overflows and none of the four threads do well. The other mistake is to transfer a person (who is loyal to the company and performing well) to a place where the company needs them, but it happens to not be in sync with the competencies or interests of the person. This is a guaranteed way of making the person leave. Because in that moment, you are feeling bullish about the person and about the prospects of the company and not seeing clearly. These are not easy mistakes to avoid.

Promoting People to their Level of Incompetence

In 1969, Peter and Raymond Hull wrote a book called *The Peter Principle*, in which they observed that people in a hierarchy tend to rise to their 'level of incompetence'.[1] In other words, a team member keeps getting promoted based on their success in previous roles until they reach a level at which they are no longer competent, as the skills required in one job do not necessarily match with the other. So now the team member is in a role in which they are not competent. Andy Grove, in his book *High Output Management*,[2] says that this situation is largely unavoidable. But what is possible is that once you know a person has hit that point, find him/her something else to do outside your company. Don't let them hang there. Otherwise everyone else will assume their competence level to be sufficient for that role—you want to avoid that completely. This value was something that took us years to realize.

Plucking Targets Out of Thin Air

Start-ups are full of optimism and it is easy to set a target which you will miss by a mile. That is disheartening for the team at the end of the year. In our initial years, we would say we want to grow five times more—now, let us do it. We would make a plan around it, work hard and still fall really short. The thing we missed doing was not listening to the on-ground folks and not understanding the real difficulties. Over the years we started a system where targets were set through both upward and downward systems. We would think about what we wanted to do in the following year and break it down into how it could be achieved. At the same time, we would ask the sales folks to share the maximum of what they thought they could do in the coming year. This exercise led to a place where the targets were stretched but achievable—a happy place to be in.

Some of the Things We Got Right

Not Capping Sales Incentives

In a lot of companies, we have seen that incentives are capped as a percentage of the total compensation. We think this is a bad strategy.

Let's say you pay a salesperson Rs 10 lakh per annum and cap the variable salary at 20 per cent, i.e. Rs 2 lakh per annum. Then during the discussion on target setting for the coming year, the incentives of the team member and the company are not aligned. Now, because the team member wants to make the entire 20 per cent of a potential bonus, they will set a lower annual target so that they can easily achieve it. As leadership, you will try to increase it so that the company can grow faster. But they will resist. By capping the incentive at 20 per cent of the salary, the interests are not aligned any more. On the other hand, if you had said that the salesperson can earn a certain percentage of the sales revenue that he brings in, and that that percentage will keep going up as the person brings in more revenue, the person will set high benchmarks for himself, which is a win-win for the company. At CoCubes, we followed three levels of incentives: Case 1, Case 2 and Case 3. In the last one, the salesperson could make almost 80 per cent of his salary as bonus, and the best ones repeatedly did.

Asking People What They Want

Ask people what salary they want. Most people are reasonable most of the time. Sometimes they are not, and that is okay. We then explain why what they are saying doesn't seem reasonable to us and, if we are on different pages, help them in their next move and part ways. If we have made a mistake, we correct it and update the pay. At the very least, everything is out in the open; they are not chatting with their colleagues about how unfair the process is, how they are worth more, and so on.

Giving Thumb Rules for Reviews

By setting some thumb rules for reviews, you help the entire company understand what to expect from them. This also gives cover to your leads before they go into a review conversation. For us, thumb rules would be things like: 'At CoCubes, we intend to be in the 80–120 per cent of the market salary range. We are building a good company, one built on good fundamentals, and we believe good people will continue to work with us at that level.'

Another thumb rule was that there would be some exceptions, may be for 1 per cent of the population. This allows for one-time corrections and situations where normal rules of business might not apply.

Being Allowed to Share Your Salary with Others

If you have been in a job earlier, then you know that everyone knows everyone else's salaries, even though the company doesn't want them to. So why create this friction in the first place? An HR rule which discourages people from discussing salaries creates disengagement by making people believe that perhaps they are not being paid fairly. Why else would the company not want people to know all the salaries?

At CoCubes, we treated our team members as adults. We didn't go as far as Semco,[3] where everyone decides their own salaries (within a range, of course) and the same is publicly displayed to the entire organization. But we told people that they could reveal their salaries to anyone they wanted to. There was no company policy on it. A survey of 71,000 people done by Payscale concluded that 82 per cent of the team members were okay with being underpaid, as long as they knew why. There were times when CoCubes also made mistakes in the review process, and we were happy to correct them. Overall, we wanted to be in a place where we had nothing to hide.

eight

if we succeed,
what will you make?
setting up a review system

The Goal of the Review Process

In most companies, the goal of the review process is to evaluate the performance of an individual in the previous year. This is misguided. If the performance was poor, the person shouldn't be in the company any more. And if the performance was good, then it is best to spend time talking about how to ensure the following:

- That the company understands the dreams of each team member.
- That the team member knows about the goals of the company for the coming year.
- That both are excited about achieving these together.

The entire process should focus on improvements and initiatives with a positive tone—a tool to encourage and motivate. Ratings traditionally have been about looking in the rear-view mirror. The focus, however, should be on looking ahead. If this outcome can be achieved at the end of reviews, the job has been well done.

So the review process is a way to align the company formally to a single vision. In a start-up, the goals keep changing frequently, and reviews are a great way to ensure that everyone is on the same page and hence prioritizing the same things. This leads to people being able to choose the right things to work on each day.

Evolving Our Review System

I remember that during the first review cycle, Vibhore and I were discussing how much the salaries should increase by; we didn't know what the right number was. The only agreement we could come to was that for good performers it should increase by enough so that it makes a material difference to them. This simple philosophy has stood the test of time over the last ten years.

In our earliest reviews, we asked everyone to rate themselves on a scale of 1 to 10. Then we went on to have a discussion on where we felt they were. We found out quite soon that without trying to define what each number meant, it was useless to try and come to a common conclusion for each person. If a team member felt that they were an 8 out of 10, and the lead felt they were at 7, there is no way one could logically conclude this discussion as there was no objectivity. 1 to 10 was too minute a scale to try and define.

188 LET'S BUILD A COMPANYLET'S BUILD A COMPANY

So we decided to move to a rating system where one's performance was rated on the following categories:

- Below expectation (BE)
- Meets expectation (ME)
- Exceeds expectation (EE)
- Rock star (RS)

This helped and worked till the time we were growing and doing well as a company. But when we were in a slump, the question of an increase in the salaries of people who were performing well created a problem. In a small team, where the outcome was company performance, how could compensation be increased if the company was not doing well?

So we introduced a metric for company goals as well. We split the annual target revenue numbers into Cases 1, 2 and 3.

Now, we were in a position, at the start of a cycle, to be able to define for each person or team what level of performance was expected from them and what performance was expected by the company. We then used it to create a matrix, or what we refer to as 'the Grid', and plug the approximate increments one could expect in each box.

The Grid: Expected increments depending on where the company landed

Company Performance	Case 3	15%	25%	40%
	Case 2	10%	15%	25%
	Case 1	5%	7.50%	10%
		ME	EE	RS
		Individual Performance		

On the company front, the metrics were quite clear and objective. In the early years, they could be goals on new users and engagement metrics, and in later years these became actual revenue numbers.

But it was still important to be able to define what BE, ME, EE and RS meant for each role in the company. This exercise took time but was important.

If We Succeed, What Will You Make?

People make or break a start-up. This is because before one has product or customers, the only thing you have are the people. And when these team members work together, they can create magic. To make this magic happen, a founder should be able to communicate three things clearly to everyone in the company:

- What is the goal of the company.
- What is expected of the person.
- What will the person get if the above two are achieved.

Many founders define the first two clearly but miss the third one, which is the critical one. That is what each person in your start-up wants to ask, and if we don't clarify that, we risk losing them giving their best every day.

At CoCubes, every year, we would implement the following process to ensure that the company and team members were in sync:

- *Step 1: Decide on our overall guidelines for salaries*: These guidelines generally remained constant over the years and were like our best practices.

- *Step 2: Decide the goals*: Remember that your company is unique; you don't need to follow an annual cycle. If in the start you want to align people to a six-month goal, go ahead and do it. Just keep in mind the cost of time in conducting a review.

- *Step 3: Outline the performance expected from each function/ person to meet goals.*

- *Step 4: Make the Grid for:*

  o Fixed compensation
  o Variable component (bonus, incentive)
  o ESOP

- *Step 5: Share with the team*: Once this is done, ensure that each person in the team understands the goals, the expectations and, finally, the monetary outcome for them.

After this we would create a review form for everyone and their leads to fill up. This form also included space for inputs from each individual on all the different functions they had worked with during the year.

Once both the reviews were filled, the leads and the individual could see the mutually filled forms. A conversation would happen between the two parties and a final form would be filled, which was followed by a final review conversation.

Time Well Spent

Deciding the metrics for each function and each individual takes time. But this is time well spent. Even if this means that the leader and the HR team are spending thirty minutes per person in deciding the right metric. The benefit is in the increased efficiency and alignment of about 2250 hours that the person will spend in the company over the following one year.

nine

creating an owner mindset

Having never managed people before in our lives, building and leading a team was a new experience. Between Vibhore and myself, the maximum we had done in terms of management was managing a team of sophomores as a Techfest manager. Attracting people, negotiating salaries, measuring output, promotions, all of these were new to us. And like everyone else, we learnt by failing again and again.

There were a few quirks we started with:

- We called every person a team member. We never addressed anyone as an employee.
- We called every manager a 'lead'. We stated that we didn't want managers within the company, we wanted leaders.

An Employee or a Team Member?

All through the years, we tried hard to not create any segregation between the leader and the lead. And this started from the top. We always thought of ourselves as team members with a lot of equity, and we communicated this again and again in our discussions with the team. An employee is deemed to be someone who is working for someone else. It *feels* like consensual modern-day slavery. In Hindi, a *naukar* (servant) does *naukari*, and in English, an employee does a job. I know it is not as black and white as this. But if we spoke to any of our friends, they would think of their job in this fashion. Their mindset was that they were employees: What could they do except working hard?

Through their policies and actions, companies make people feel this way every single day. But as the younger generation, we didn't want to be naukars and we didn't want any employees. We even consulted lawyers to see if we could replace the term 'employee' in the employment agreements with 'team members' or something else. Due to legal reasons that didn't work out. But we wanted to ensure that folks who worked at CoCubes didn't feel like employees but like team members.

Managers or Leaders?

After starting the company, when we met a relative at a family function, the general metric of evaluation of our company would be: '*Kitne log hai?* [How many people does your company employ?]' 'Managing people' in India is considered to be a glorified task. In our short stints at other companies, we had realized that we didn't want to be managed. We would fret over why MBAs had been hired to manage a team of analysts? How could X enjoy or take responsibility for his work when they know that

Y is supposed to manage everything? Thinking like this sucked the joy out of me, and I believe it sucks the joy out of anyone who is told that they need to be managed. We wanted people to take ownership of and responsibility for their tasks. We wanted them to figure out the 'how' of the work themselves. And, if stuck, just walk over and talk to their lead or anyone else in their team. As a lead, the key priority was to explain to team members 'why something is being done' as opposed to 'here is what you need to do'. This led to an 'owner' mindset within CoCubes which served the company well and built an organization where folks took ownership of their work.

Don't Compare People

People hate to be compared to each other. When we started, we used to do it often. There is generally a star person in each function, and it is easy to set them as a benchmark and compare everyone to them. This almost always backfires because:

- Everyone has an ego (big or small), and nobody likes being told that the other person is better than them.
- The person to whom one is being compared gets overconfident over time.
- Most importantly, you haven't told the person in question anything to help them improve. You have simply said, 'Why can't you be as good as that other person?'

It is always better to give someone objective and actionable feedback rather than a comparison. If we want people to learn from each other, it is best to say, 'Can you talk to Deepak and ask him for tips on how to improve your pitch?'

No Individual Awards

In our entire twelve years of running CoCubes, we never singled out an individual for an award. There is a difference between an award and praise. Praise is never in comparison to someone else. But if you award someone with the title of 'Best Account Manager' or 'Employee of the Month', what you implicitly say is that everyone else has done a lesser job than this person, that their contributions are not worthy of an award. Over time, this leads to a workplace where:

- You give too many awards, so the entire purpose of making someone feel special is lost in the process. And it becomes a useless exercise.
- As the organization grows, each leader tries to push people from their team to get the award that month. And then if they don't get the award, they have to go back and try to explain to their team member why he or she had not done as good a job to deserve it. This fuels discontent both at the bottom and top and leads to jealousy.

At CoCubes, we were quick to spot and praise positive action. We would also get the team together (or write an email) saying that CoCubes had done a brilliant job in delivering this project and congratulating 'everyone involved' in making it possible. When we do this, everyone knows which 'folks' are being referred to and they, too, get the message that teamwork is valued at CoCubes.

Offering a Career Path

There are a lot of situations where big companies have an edge over start-ups. One such instance is the ability to offer a well-defined career. They are able to tell a person where they can reach if they stick with the company for ten years; that becoming a vice president takes nine years and four promotions. I say that this is an edge because it affords visibility to a team member. But at the same time, this can be frustrating in a large company because you know that no matter how hard and smart you work, becoming a vice president will still take nine years.

Once we had grown a little bigger, team members began to come to us and ask how their careers would grow. And invariably our question to them would be: *How do you want it to grow?* The first few years this would stump people because what we were saying was that you need to decide where you want it to go. Within CoCubes, when we were growing fast during the initial years, there were always openings in product, sales, operations and marketing. Name it and you have it. So what area did the team member really want to grow in? We wanted them to feel that they had ownership of their careers and to discuss with us what they really wanted to do.

At the same time, getting to such a level of ownership takes a few years. This is because till class ten, the path was nice and clean. Most people would choose between medical or another stream. Then, if they got a good rank, they would opt for computer science. It takes time for people to come out of this mindset. To realize that they have the choice of taking ownership of their career paths. And that sometimes those career paths would lie within CoCubes and sometimes outside it. Both are okay. What we wanted to ensure was that everyone working in CoCubes believed that their destiny was in their hands and that they felt they were in charge.

Titles

In his article, Borowitz argues between two methods—Andreessen vs Zuckerberg.[1] While Andreessen believed that a title is one of those things that is easy to give, and that one should give people the highest title possible to keep them happy socially, Zuckerberg deploys titles that are significantly lower than the industry standard. He wants titles to be meaningful and reflect who has influence within the organization. Keeping in mind the few hundreds of people CoCubes had, we chose the Andreessen method. It also fit in with our philosophy of letting people take their fate in to their own hands. If someone would ask, what would my title be, we would in turn ask them what they would want it to be. Do you want to be the CEO? That generally calmed people down. They got the message that titles in this firm were not all-important.

Some sales folks preferred 'Senior Manager', while another wanted to be 'Regional Lead'. While this seems like a free-for-all, it wasn't. Once people understood that titles within the company had no value, they chose them only to have some social value; and they chose it carefully to ensure that they could pull it off. This also provided useful feedback during the interview process on the kind of person we were interviewing. There were a couple of times when a person took on a title too big for them. This generally happened with more experienced people who wanted to look senior by designation too. In almost all such cases, the person didn't work out. A person who spent too much time fussing over the exact designation and where their office seat would be wasn't a great fit for CoCubes. Over time, we learnt to filter out such folks.

Unsurprisingly, everyone wanted to be known as a manager. Which was okay as long as they understood that the role meant managing the work, not people. So a 'Manager–Corporate Accounts' would be managing multiple accounts and not people. But to a client this conveyed that the person handling their account was a manager and not a 'Junior Associate'. This helped a lot optically. No client wants to be saddled with a junior person. Every client (big or small) wants to deal with someone senior enough to get their work done within the firm. Having a manager associated with external-facing roles helped tremendously to reduce the burden of attending to client requests for interface with senior folks within the company. So the person who was now a manager was happy, the client was happy and CoCubes was also able to save the bandwidth of its senior resources. All of this also inculcated a feeling of taking ownership in the company.

We Formed a Lead Code

In a start-up, the value of organizational knowledge with the early members is high. As the start-up grows, these members end up being in positions of leading other people—a position they are sometimes not emotionally ready for. Most of them are first-time leaders. As our team grew, we had several first-time managers, so we created a 'lead code' to ensure that:

- The lead understood what was expected from them.
- The team being led was on board with what they should expect from a lead.

This helped us to make sure that everyone was aligned with the kind of culture we wanted to create within the company.

Our lead code looked like this:

- Know the people reporting to you personally.
- Meet their family, understand and appreciate their concerns.
- Understand their goals and aspirations.
- Participate in celebrations: weddings and birthdays are compulsory.
- You work for whoever reports to you, your role is to help them achieve their goals.
- If the goals of whoever reports to you are not aligned with the company's, help them plan their career and help the company find a replacement.
- Criticize actions, not people. The person is not incorrect, the action is.
- Integrity comes first. This, once breached, is the end of the road.
- Consciously find reasons to praise the person.

At the end of the day, a team member working on something can think of their work in two ways:

- I have to do this because my boss will ask me about it in the evening.

- I have to do this because the work I am doing is of value to the company.

This is an important distinction. Ask yourself, what feeling does your company leave people with?

C. Some Learnings

one

the importance of the market

When we started CoCubes, entrepreneurship was not considered cool. Parents wouldn't have married their daughters off to entrepreneurs. In our batch of 440 people from IIT Bombay, we were only the second set of guys to become entrepreneurs and raise venture capital. Gagan Goyal, who built Thinklabs and is now a partner with India Quotient, was the first.

As first-time entrepreneurs, it took us a lot of time to realize that we operated in an industry that was known formally as the 'HR-tech industry'. An industry, which as we later realized, venture capitalists didn't like too much (and with good reason). It also dawned on us that selling to companies in India was not considered lucrative. Lastly, we understood that the B2B industry was not fashionable. All of these were foreign concepts to us when we were twenty-four years old. We didn't think about this when we started the company. We picked an idea that we really cared about. The idea happened to be in the B2B, education and the HR-tech market! A deadly combination.

Even before leaving our jobs, on weekends, I tried to meet potential customers. After each meeting, I would write a note to Vibhore and Dhayan (who, at that point, was looking to start CoCubes with us). Below are the notes from one of my first meetings.

3 November 2007

Guys,
Just visited a college in Kharar, near Chandigarh. This is what I've gathered:

- *The training and placement officer can be an old and difficult guy to deal with.*
- *He can be locked in his room by the students.*
- *They are willing to share student data.*
- *Out of their batch of 450 passing out, only 50 satisfy the criteria that companies put out.*
- *Their current focus is on getting more admissions (which is indirectly linked to placements).*
- *Internet penetration exists but relying on it would be foolish.*
- *MBAs from the college get paid Rs 11,000 as starting salaries.*

Looking back, I think this meeting told me everything that I needed to know about the college market. There was a consistent pattern across the country: placement officers were generally elderly gentleman with inertia; the college owners were generally street-savvy businessmen, usually not from an educational background, and colleges weren't their only business.

Getting admissions and jobs were the only two priorities for the students. Jobs were a priority because parents were getting their children to study engineering only for this reason. Therefore, it mattered to the college as well. The more successful campus placements they organized, the more admissions they got. Employability was low. In every college, not more than 20 per cent of the students were employable, and the starting salaries for most students, even after an engineering and MBA degree, were low.

We did not need to spend five more years after that to come to the same conclusion. We couldn't change the number of jobs being created in the country, we couldn't change the salary being offered and we couldn't change the expectations that parents and students had from the college. If we were really focused as entrepreneurs to solve the problem of jobs, of helping students make careers, we would have shifted the model back then, because working with colleges would have always been a slow process and the delivery of jobs would have always been difficult.

But it took years for this reality to sink in. We had named our company CoCubes, connecting colleges and companies. We had committed to colleges. Making this big a change was something we were mentally not ready for. So we went on trying to hire better sales guys, trying different models that could work with colleges—internships rather than jobs, connecting with companies rather than placements, guest lectures, and so on—but nothing worked at scale.

If we could go back, we would take the hard call of changing the market rather than trying to optimize it. Or we would try being in the same market but working directly with students. We discussed it back then too, but we had already gone down the path of building a login for placement officers and creating an entire platform that helped colleges optimize placements. Throwing a year's effort away was a hard call. We didn't do that. And so we threw five years and two rounds of venture capital away.

Today, I meet so many entrepreneurs who reach out to me and ask: *How can the sales cycle with colleges be reduced?* My answer is simple: *It can't.* It is possible to optimize the process. You can have a better salesperson, you can do better marketing and your sales pitch can be more efficient, but at the end of the day, it will take three to six months and three to four meetings for you to sign up a customer *if* you have a good product. Till the time the market changes, i.e. until the expectations of parents and students from the colleges change, or the owners of colleges start focusing on teaching, what will excite a college in the first place won't change. Jobs and admissions are still the top priority for colleges.

I think the market is singularly the most important external thing that can make or break the company.

The Thing about Markets Is That They Change

When we started working with colleges in 2007, students didn't have smartphones. Later, if someone had a smartphone, they didn't have a fast Internet connection. The idea that a student could download an app and apply online for a job through their phone was laughable. All the student data in colleges was stored in Excel files. In most Excel files, the fields for mobile-phone numbers were empty. So each step of the journey took a lot of time, and some of these were things that we couldn't solve; we could only wait for the market to evolve. Mobile phones had to become cheaper, 4G had to emerge and then become affordable for everyone. If we were to start CoCubes today, we wouldn't do the college model at all. We would find a way to reach students directly. We would build something that attracts students and helps solve the employability gap.

In 2012, we were faced with a similar market situation when we decided to start selling assessments to corporates. I remember sitting in front of an HR person, pitching our assessments, and they replied, 'Why should I pay you Rs 200 for an assessment when I can just take a printout for 50 paise?' I also remember meeting Hitesh Oberoi, the CEO of Naukri.com, and he told me that what we were offering was not good business for him. There is no market size, because the top three companies together make less than Rs 50 crore in revenue.

He was right about how things were in the past and at the time we spoke to him. But I don't think he was right about the future. In three years, we went from most HR people doubting us to online assessments being accounted for in their budgets. Today, the top-three corporate assessment companies in India do more than Rs 200 crore in revenue, and all of them are profitable and growing at a rate of more than 30 per cent. What really changed in the market was the wave of digitization. Every CEO wanted their company and each function to move to digital so that it could be measured. In that wave, digitization assessments also picked up and became more popular.

The reason I bring this up is that a lot of times, there is little that one can do to change a market which is not ready (the exception being large consumer markets where billions of dollars can be put in to create the market). You can change your idea and your company. But it is much more difficult to build in a market when it is not ready for your product. In such cases, even having a product market fit leads to mediocre outcomes—which is totally avoidable!

two

the importance of organizational knowledge

I once read a beautiful article on Africa. It talked about the countries in the African continent that did well after gaining political independence and those that didn't. What was eye-opening for me was the reason that was identified for the countries doing well. The countries in question hadn't asked their white population to leave after gaining independence. Actually, they asked them to stay; the leaders of the new republics understood that they didn't yet know how to run the country. How to produce wealth for the country? How to ensure that the right infrastructure was built? More than ever before they needed the help of experts to do it. And if the experts were white, so be it.

This approach resonated with me. There is a lot of value in organizational knowledge. More so when the company is small, and the processes and documentation are less. The person who handled finance at CoCubes, Nishant Ahuja, had been around for the last eight years. He had joined in a different role, entering data into Excel, then generating invoices and then finally moving to finance. If there was a query from the income tax department or the Reserve Bank of India, he would remember what caused the problem. While working with CAs and company secretaries, he was able to guide them on how we were recognizing revenue, why the head of a certain expenditure should change, and so on. He was also able to answer any queries from old employees about full and final settlements.

Then there was Ankur Jindal. He had joined CoCubes as an intern in 2007. He had grown to become the head of operations by 2014. He knew the ins and outs of each account, every operational glitch we faced, why we had lost a certain account, what problems we had faced in which year, and so on. He was like a magnet who had all the stories of CoCubes within him and was someone that people looked up to. Having a person like him in the organization also provides a sense of security and stability to the new folks who join. They see a person who has grown from scratch within the company and carries the knowledge of everything there is to know about working there, and he is willing to share that information.

Veterans in the organization get called on by new sales folks, or by product managers, who want to know what had happened earlier with an account or a failed product, or in a market. This is invaluable. It is impossible to document such knowledge, and if you don't have folks with tenure in your company, this responsibility generally ends up falling on the founders. Just as the African nations found out, we too realized that having people with organizational knowledge, who are still hungry to perform, is a game changer.

three

---

getting an office

Don't get a new office with your investor money.

If only we had seventy bucks (i.e. a dollar) for every time this advice has been given to an entrepreneur and consequently been ignored by him or her! And we are admittedly a part of that list.

After keeping the rent in check for a long time, we had gone on to take up a fancy office. So what do you think happened? Why does the simple advice of refraining from getting a fancy office continue to be ignored?

The answer lies in the answer to another question: Why is capital raised from the investor in the first place?

Why Is Capital Raised from the Investors?

When the deck is made for an investor, a slide detailing how one would use the money is mandatory. In almost all cases, the pie is split into:

- Building the product.
- Marketing to acquire customers.
- Hiring people.

These are the right places to spend money. This doesn't include renting an office. But as an entrepreneur, one believes that to get the best people we need a fancy office, and for existing team members to do well, they should have enough space to work.

No doubt, hiring definitely becomes easier after getting a nice office. But that also sends the founder into a lull because you no longer have to convince people about the vision you have for your company. This is dangerous because in many cases you hire people who might not actually believe in your vision but join for many other reasons.

What Kind of People Does One Attract with a Fancy Office?

Risk-averse People

The first kind of people who get attracted to a fancy office are risk-averse people. When someone joins your company not because they believe in what you are doing but because you have a nice office with a coffee machine, lounge chairs and a big pantry, they do not constitute better talent for you. This is because there is a possibility that in your journey the fancy office may go away, and when that happens, so will many of those folks who joined looking at the fancy office. The daily life of a start-up is an unending slog. Start-ups are risky both for the entrepreneur and for the person joining them. While the ride is enjoyable and your learning curve will be high, anything can happen, and this should be made clear to the person upfront.

People Who Believe That Things Are Solved

Many people don't understand what a start-up life is all about. They don't know how much of a struggle it is to solve things fundamentally—to take a problem and find a solution to it, end to end. This has generally never been taught in schools and colleges, and is not encouraged by parents either. When people see your office and find everything shiny and new, that the coffee machine works and that the chair is soft, they believe their needs have been met. And that this will be like any other job. But it isn't. The money you have just raised is to help find solutions, and to find them fast. For that, you need a person who is comfortable with ambiguity, who is comfortable with things that are broken, who likes fixing stuff. Not a person who believes things are solved.

People Who Value Comfort and Money

When a prospective employee whom you have invited for a final interview sees a lounge chair, they imagine what their life will be like after joining the company. They see themselves joining the company and sitting on that chair with a coffee mug in their hand, sipping away while working on a MacBook. It's a great picture for the 'gram. Well, here's the truth: start-up is real life. And if you have just bought jet fuel from a venture capitalist, they expect to see speed. So people who value comfort will join and either be comfortable, or, if pushed hard, will leave. Some will have the self-discipline to push themselves, but most will not. And for such people, if the interiors of an office are enough to convince them to join, a good hike in another company is also good enough for them to leave.

Maybe at the late stages of a start-up, once the product market fit has been achieved, some metrics have been set and you have a clearer path to building a valuable company, it becomes important to hire folks who value stability. Hence, a fancy office becomes important. You hire people and then convert them to your vision. Your start-up is now running more steadily, and they will have time to sit on the lounge chair, read a newspaper and sip on some coffee while contributing productively to the company. But that is simply not the case when you raise your first angel or venture capital round.

Having a fancy office also impacts older employees, including yourself. As you invite your friends to come around to see it, they are wowed; when your parents come by to see it and hug you, you also feel that you have arrived, that you can rest a little. But the only thing that has happened is that you now have all the resources needed to fulfil your vision and that you need to double down and work harder.

There are companies that, after getting venture capital, got big offices and have gone on to do well. The thing to remember is that they have done well *in spite* of taking the call to get a fancy office, not *because* of it.

four

cocubes after the sale

After selling the company in 2016, we started to get used to working as a part of a larger company. We found people at Aon, the largest HR consulting firm in the world, to be nice and accommodating. The day we announced the deal, they welcomed us by throwing a party and inviting leaders from around the world. They allowed us to stay and grow out of our existing office rather than pushing us to merge with the big corporate office. This gave us the flexibility and freedom to continue growing and delivering to the clients in the way we had been doing earlier.

Having the brand of Aon with us helped in selling to large companies who were looking for a single partner to implement things globally. Aon gave us access to the new solutions and, together, this became a strong appeal for clients.

Because Aon had a global presence, a lot of people from CoCubes were able to travel to different parts of the world and work with colleagues and clients from all over. This is an experience that we would have been unable to provide on our own, as CoCubes.

A lot of times, team members in CoCubes complained that things were changing very slowly. Financial decisions were being made slowly, the salary hikes were a little less and legal approvals also took time. We explained to them that this was bound to happen. As an entrepreneur, one can't sell the company and continue to believe that it will be run the same way. That would be quite stupid. Someone else owns the company, and we need to find a good way of working together. That is the message we gave to the senior leadership and other team members. We had no senior-level attrition in the two years after selling the company. All of the top leadership continued to stay, as did most of the other folks. This had been possible because of the transparency with which we ran our office. People knew what to expect and we delivered on our word.

A thing we are happy about is that CoCubes continues to do well as a business despite us. It continues to grow and create opportunities for the team members working there, while creating wealth for Aon.

Vibhore and I exited the company in April 2019. At the end of 2019 Vibhore started OneBanc.ai—a neo bank. Vibhore has been passionate about the fintech sector, so he has gone in that direction. Not running our next company together has been a hard decision, but I want to spend a large part of my time solving problems in the people space. Education for young kids interests me; creating something for a teenager, which enables him/her to decide what they want to do with their life, is another hard nut to crack, as is the issue of how to help someone find the next step in their career.

Along with working on what we want to do next, we started angel investing and also working with other entrepreneurs in their journeys.

In our time with CoCubes, we saw two recessions. Today, in 2020, because of COVID-19, we are all seeing tough times again. But sometimes the best ideas, the best efforts happen in tough external situations.

We hope you find, in your life, whatever brings out the best in you, and that you have the courage to see it through.

And if there is any way we can help, drop us a line on www.letsbuildacompany.com.

appendix 1

graphs

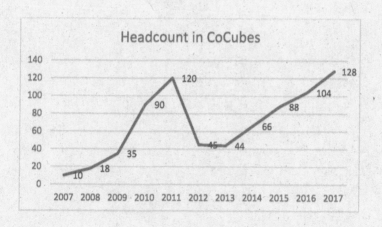

Source: Public year-end tax and Provident Fund filing records of CoCubes

notes

PART I: STARTING A START-UP

Chapter 1: The Idea of CoCubes

1. By the time we graduated, my CPI (cumulative performance index) was 8.9 and Vibhore's was 8.5. In the long run, I got ahead, although Vibhore attributes this to civil being easier than electronics, a claim I haven't agreed to so far. Because, tomorrow, he could then turn around and say that sales and operations is easier than product and tech. So, as co-founders, we have let this matter be open-ended.

Chapter 3: Getting Things Done

1. Name changed to protect privacy.

Chapter 4: Money for Our Idea

1. Mark Sweney, 'Pearson buys controlling stake in TutorVista for $127m', *Guardian*, 18 January 2011, https://www.theguardian.com/business/2011/jan/18/pearson-tutorvista-india.
2. 'Ola Electric gets $250m funding from SoftBank', *Economic Times*, 3 July 2019, https://economictimes.indiatimes.com/small-biz/startups/newsbuzz/ola-electric-gets-250m-funding-from-softbank/articleshow/70050081.cms.

Chapter 6: Raising the VC Round

1. 'Why Indian middle class families don't encourage aspiring entrepreneurs', Inc42, 27 April 2013, https://inc42.com/entrepreneurship/why-indian-middle-class-families-dont-encourage-aspiring-entrepreneurs/.

PART II: FOR THE ENTREPRENEUR IN YOU

A. *Personal Life*

Chapter 1: The Married Life of an Entrepreneur

1. Bhakti, my wife, has specifically asked me to add that I have started checking my phone again and paying less attention to her. I keep telling her, it's time for the second start-up.

B. *The Biggest Asset: People*

Chapter 1: Building Culture

1. 'Tony Hsieh', Wikipedia, https://en.wikipedia.org/wiki/Tony_Hsieh.

2. Ben Horowitz, 'A Good Place to Work', Andreessen Horowitz (a16z), 18 August 2012, https://a16z.com/2012/08/18/a-good-place-to-work/.

3. Paul Bielby, *Simply the Best: 500 Football Tips for Youngsters* (London: John Blake Publishing).

Chapter 2: Creating the Culture at CoCubes

1. Jason Fried and David Heinemeier Hansson, *ReWork* (New York: Crown Publishing, 2010).

Chapter 4: Common Mistakes Made while hiring

1. Brian Fink, 'The Only Thing That Matters Is the Team', LinkedIn, 10 July 2017, https://www.linkedin.com/pulse/only-thing-matters-team-brian-fink.

Chapter 5: Hiring Slow. Firing Fast.

1. Mark Suster, 'Startup Mantra: Hire Fast, Fire Fast', *Both Sides of the Table* (blog), 27 May 2011, https://bothsidesofthetable.com/startup-mantra-hire-fast-fire-fast-524ac1cac877.

Chapter 7: Common People-Management Mistakes We Made, and Some Things We Got Right

1. 'Peter principle', Wikipedia, https://en.wikipedia.org/wiki/Peter_principle.

2. Ben Horowitz, 'Andy', Andreessen Horowitz (a16z), 13 November 2015, https://a16z.com/2015/11/13/high-output-management/.

3. Ian Borges, 'What Happens When Employees Choose Their Own Salaries', Journal Leadwise, 4 December 2017, https://

journal.leadwise.co/what-happens-when-employees-choose-theirown-salaries-d4e210ad8db.

Chapter 9: Creating an Owner Mindset

4. Ben Horowitz, 'Titles and Promotions', Andreessen Horowitz (a16z), 16 March 2011, https://a16z.com/2011/03/16/titles-and-promotions/.